AQA GCSE

GCSE Revision GUIDE

Business Studies

Neil Denby

D0314034

Philip Allan Updates, an imprint of Hodder Education, an Hachette UK company, Market Place, Deddington, Oxfordshire OX15 0SE

Orders

Bookpoint Ltd, 130 Milton Park, Abingdon, Oxfordshire OX14 4SB
tel: 01235 827720
fax: 01235 400454
e-mail: uk.orders@bookpoint.co.uk
Lines are open 9.00 a.m.–5.00 p.m., Monday to Saturday, with a 24-hour message answering service. You can also order through the Philip Allan Updates website: www.philipallan.co.uk

© Philip Allan Updates 2010
ISBN 978-1-4441-0776-0

First printed 2010
Impression number   5   4   3   2   1
Year   2014   2013   2012   2011   2010

Printed in Italy

Hachette UK's policy is to use papers that are natural, renewable and recyclable products and made from wood grown in sustainable forests. The logging and manufacturing processes are expected to conform to the environmental regulations of the country of origin.

P01658

Contents

Introduction

How to revise

Revision is not just about remembering, but about being able to apply what you have remembered to business situations. You should, therefore, make sure that you do not just learn facts, but know how a business would use them in its decision making. There are very few questions that will ask you for straightforward knowledge.

10 tips for effective revision

1 Start revising in plenty of time. You may have to revisit some topics at the last minute, but you should try to make sure there are only a few of these.
2 Have a set time and place, where you cannot be disturbed, for your revision sessions.
3 Plan your revision carefully — make sure you leave enough time to cover everything.
4 Plan short-term targets — 'I will have learnt *xxx* by *xxx*.' These show you are making progress and help to motivate you.
5 Do not do too much! Your brain needs regular rests in order to be able to process and store information properly.
6 Revise topics three times. This will help to put the knowledge into your long-term memory.
7 Make sure your revision is active — make notes, use spider diagrams, pictograms and mind maps, write raps or lyrics. Sound and visual reminders are usually better than just words.
8 Think about using new technology. You could make a podcast of a revision topic and listen to it on your MP3 player.
9 Practise applying your knowledge to business situations. Use the questions in this book to practise your examination technique. Make sure you draw on all the relevant information, not just a single topic.
10 Revise with someone else — then you can test each other, compare notes, etc.

How to use this book

Each topic in the book is short and contains the basic knowledge you will need to pass at GCSE. In each topic there are a number of features.

- *What the specification requires.* This tells you the sort of knowledge that the specification needs you to know, and steers you in the direction of the types of question that can be asked.

- *In brief.* This states the knowledge requirement in a couple of sentences. For last-minute refreshers, this is what you will need.

- *Revision notes.* This feature outlines the area of knowledge that it is absolutely essential for you to know about each topic.

- *Speak the language.* This gives the key terms and definitions that you will need for a particular topic. In all GCSE business examinations, there are marks for using the correct technical language. These are highlighted in the text.

- *In a nutshell.* This contains the key points from the topic as a bullet list.

- *Boost your grade.* This feature tells you how to access AO1 knowledge marks or how to move from AO1 to AO2 explanation and context marks or from AO2 to AO3 analysis, recommendation and judgement marks.

- *Test yourself.* This provides a short test on the content of all or part of the topic. It takes the form of multiple-choice questions, missing word questions or tests that you can self-set.

At the end of each section, you will find a longer question, a set of multiple-choice questions or a similar exercise to test your knowledge. At the end of each unit, you will find a full practice examination paper, just like the one that you will sit for your GCSE.

Suggested answers to all the questions are available online at: **www.hodderplus.co.uk/philipallan**.

AQA GCSE Business Studies

The AQA GCSE Business Studies qualification is not one GCSE, but several. There is a 'suite' of units to choose from and different ways to achieve the qualification. The choices that you make can lead you to a short-course qualification (half a GCSE), a full-course single GCSE qualification, or a double award (two GCSEs) Applied Business qualification. In each case, the core unit, and the first one likely to be taught, is Unit 1.

Unit 1 Setting up a business

Unit 1 is 'Setting up a business'. It covers the initial start-up of a business and concentrates on small businesses. It focuses on giving you the skills and knowledge to start your own business, should you wish to do so. It looks at the factors that might help a small business to succeed, and at the various problems that such a business might face. It shows where the solutions to those problems might be found. It also shows that businesses have an impact on many other groups — called stakeholders. These include the people and organisations that lend them money, the communities in which they operate, the people whom they employ and, perhaps most importantly, the customers they hope to gain.

Unit 1 content

Unit 1 of the specification is covered in Unit 1 of this book. It takes you through the initial start-up of a business from first ideas to aims and objectives. Is there a gap in the market, or can one be created? It covers where you might locate the business and the stakeholders who will have an interest in it. It also shows how businesses can reduce risk of failure, whether through careful planning, limiting liability or taking on a franchise. Businesses are unlikely to succeed unless customers and potential customers know what they are selling and where. This unit therefore looks at marketing. It looks at ways for a small business to research the market on a limited budget, and at appropriate advertising and promotion. Finance for the business covers the support available from government, sources of finance and a basic understanding of financial terms and accounts. A recruitment section looks at how you would find and fill vacancies, and encourage staff to work hard, while operating within the law. Finally, knowledge of methods of production for a small business and how operations impact on customers is included.

Short or full course?

From the starting point of Unit 1, you can then decide which qualification route you wish to take. You could take the short-course GCSE by sitting an examination based on Unit 1 and producing a piece of coursework called a controlled assessment (explained on page 141). The controlled assessment is called 'Investigating Small Businesses' so, if you decide on this route, you will only learn about small businesses. This unit asks you to investigate a real small business and then present your conclusions in a business-like manner. You could then decide to continue and take the full GCSE course. You will still take an examination on Unit 1 and the controlled assessment (Unit 3), but will also be examined on Unit 2.

Unit 2 Growing as a business

Unit 2 covers the further growth and expansion of a business, so it concentrates on larger businesses and on the problems and benefits that expansion can bring. It is covered in Unit 2 of this book. Here, the emphasis is on large businesses. Many of the topics covered have similar titles to those of Unit 1, but the focus is very different. For example, when looking at raising finance, large businesses can sell shares on the stock exchange, use their own profits or sell off machinery and plant that is no longer needed. These are not options available to the small business. Larger businesses also have bigger ethical and environmental responsibilities. The growing business needs a balanced and effective marketing mix, and the emphasis here is on how it achieves this, and on how it uses the marketing mix to contribute to its success. Finance is more complex at this level, so financial tools and accounts are studied in greater detail. Large organisation structures and their problems show the importance of people. Larger structures are recognised as bringing challenges, and the final part of the specification looks at how those challenges can be overcome.

Double award

If you decide to take the double award Applied GCSE qualification, you still start with Unit 1. In addition to this, you would choose two controlled assessment units chosen from Unit 4: People in Business; Unit 5: Marketing and Customer Needs; and Unit 6: Enterprise. Because these are examined by controlled assessment (coursework), there is no real need to have to revise them, as material can be taken into the classroom to help you write your reports. They are much more about applying knowledge than remembering it. These are covered in the section on controlled assessment on page 141. In addition, you will take an examination on Business Finance. Much of the learning for this is covered in the finance sections of Unit 1 and Unit 2. Unit 7: Finance, however, covers some new ground, so this is explained on pages 122–140.

Further study

The specification is designed to get you to think about how, practically, you could become involved in business as an entrepreneur or stakeholder. It also acts as a springboard for further study at AS or A-level.

Unit 1
Setting up a business

Topic 1
Starting a business enterprise

What the specification requires

You need to learn about and understand that businesses are set up to provide those things that people want. These products may be **goods** or **services**. In most cases, businesses are set up with the intention of making a **profit**. In some cases — called **social enterprises** — they are set up to provide a service to a community.

In brief

What is a business? It is a person or group of people who find out what people want and need, and then aim to provide this. People want goods and services. Goods are basically things you can touch — ranging from food to fuel, computers to kites, telephones to toys. Services are things that are done to you or for you: for example, haircuts, delivery, entertainment, banking and communication.

Businesses decide what to sell by seeing what people want (known as **demand**) and what is not currently being supplied. If people demand something and no one is supplying it yet, this is called a **gap in the market**.

Revision notes

- Businesses are set up in order to provide the products that people need and want, but which they are not able or willing to provide for themselves.
- By providing products to the customers who want them, businesses are operating in a market.
- A market is anywhere that buyers and sellers come together to agree on the price for an amount of a product. This does not have to be a physical place: markets can take place via telephone or online.

Just one sort of market — with products, supply and demand

- A product will be either a good or a service. Goods are things that can be touched; services are done for or to a customer.
- People start businesses either to make a profit or to provide a service to a community.
- Those people who take the risk of starting a business, and provide the organisation, are called **entrepreneurs**. Their reward, if the business is a success, is profit. Profit is the surplus of income (revenue) over costs.
- Those businesses providing a community service (like charities and co-operatives) are called social enterprises.
- New businesses look for a gap in the market. A gap in the market is where a demand exists, but it is not being met. Some gaps are to provide specialist goods or services; these are called niche markets.
- Businesses with new products or ideas may be able to create a gap in the market.

Speak the language

demand — the amount of products and services customers are willing to pay for

entrepreneurs — the person who takes the risk of starting a business

gap in the market — where there is demand, but no product to fill it

goods — those things that can be touched

profit — the surplus of income (revenue) over costs

services — those things done to or for a customer

social enterprises — businesses set up to provide a service to a community

In a nutshell

* Businesses provide products to markets.
* To succeed, they need to find a gap in the market.
* Often they are set up to make a profit.
* Profit is the surplus of revenue over costs and the reward for the entrepreneur.
* Sometimes they are set up to provide a service to a community.

Boost your grade

AO1 to AO2: you are unlikely to be asked questions on 'what is a business' that require AO3-level answers. The idea of what a business is, and what it does, and an understanding of key terms like 'profit' will give you AO1 marks. For AO2 marks, you must use the business example you are given.

Test yourself

Fill in the gaps in the paragraph below.

Businesses are set up in order to provide the .... that people need and want. Businesses sell and customers buy. This is called a .... Goods are things that can be touched as opposed to things done for or to a customer, called .... Entrepreneurs start businesses either to make a .... or to provide a service to a community. Those businesses providing a community service (such as charities and co-operatives) are called ....

What the specification requires

You need to know and understand why a person starting up a business might operate as a franchisee. You need to understand that there are both advantages and disadvantages to being part of a franchise, rather than setting up an independent business.

In brief

Franchising is when a successful business decides to expand by selling the right to other businesses to set up using its ideas. A franchise is a way of starting, owning and operating a business without the high levels of risk that may be associated with other types of start-up. A franchise is a way to organise a business rather than a form of business ownership. It helps the person selling the franchise to expand and gives the person buying the franchise a much better chance of surviving and succeeding.

Revision notes

- A franchise is permission to sell a product (good or service) or brand or to use the successful format of an existing business.
- There are two key players in a **franchise**.
- The **franchisee** buys the franchise from the **franchiser** (think employer and employee to get these the right way round).

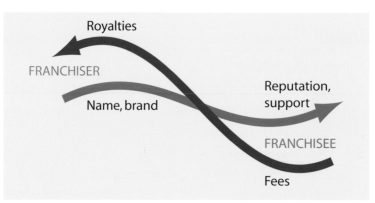

BSM instructors buy franchises from BSM

- The franchisee buys into the success of the established business. It buys the use of its name, its brand, its advertising, its reputation and its support.
- The franchiser is the seller of the franchise that has a successful product, brand or format.
- Franchisers charge a fee for the franchise and collect a **royalty**, usually based on a percentage of the annual sales of the franchisee.
- Because a franchisee is buying into a successful product, the fee for the franchise can often be high and competition to buy a franchise quite fierce.
- Franchisers may be restrictive — insisting on particular suppliers and making sure that uniforms, products and services are identical.
- The advantage to franchisees is that they buy into an established business and may receive help with products, staff, training, marketing and sales materials. They are much more likely to succeed.
- Franchisees may also gain an exclusive territory, away from competition for the same brand.
- The disadvantage is that there may be restrictions on how they can run the business.
- The advantage to the franchiser is that their idea or brand is spread. It is a way to expand the business.
- Franchisers also receive an income from the franchisee.
- One disadvantage is that a poor franchisee may harm their reputation.

Speak the language

franchise — permission to use a successful business format

franchisee — the buyer of the franchise

franchiser — the seller of the franchise

royalty — a percentage of the franchisee's income taken as payment by the franchiser

In a nutshell

* A franchise is a form of business organisation.
* Franchisees buy the right to use the franchiser's name and reputation.
* Franchisers gain by expanding their business and receiving fees.
* Franchisees gain by being much more likely to succeed.

Test yourself

Choose the most appropriate answer from the following alternatives.

1 A franchisee is **(a)** the seller of the franchise, **(b)** the buyer of the franchise, **(c)** the owner of the brand, **(d)** a customer of the franchise.

2 A royalty is **(a)** a set amount, **(b)** based on a percentage, **(c)** Burger King, **(d)** fixed each year.

3 If a franchisee harms the reputation of the franchise, this is **(a)** an advantage to the franchiser, **(b)** an advantage to the franchisee, **(c)** a disadvantage to the franchiser, **(d)** a disadvantage to the franchisee.

4 Franchises can help new businesses to **(a)** set up, **(b)** borrow money, **(c)** reduce risk, **(d)** expand.

5 Franchises can help successful businesses to **(a)** set up, **(b)** borrow money, **(c)** reduce risk, **(d)** expand.

Boost your grade

AO1 to AO2: a franchise is just one form of business ownership, but can be very appropriate to a start-up business. For AO2 marks you may be asked to explain or give reasons why a franchise may be suitable to the business you have been given. AO1 marks will be given for stating a reason (it is a successful business) and AO2 marks will be given for explaining the reason (so the new business will already be well known).

Business aims and objectives

What the specification requires

You need to know and understand the difference between **aims** and **objectives** and why a business sets them for itself. You should know the main types of aims, such as survival, profit, growth and market share. You should understand how and why a business might try to set **ethical** and **sustainable** aims. You should know how objectives are used to help measure success.

In brief

Businesses need to know whether or not they are making progress or succeeding in what they are trying to do. To find this out, they need to measure their progress. Progress can be measured by using aims and objectives. Aims are long term and shape how the business operates. Objectives are shorter term and can be used to help run the business. Progress can be measured by setting and reaching objectives.

Revision notes

- Aims are long-term goals towards which the business can work.
- Aims are often not precise; a business may, for instance, aim to be 'the customer's first choice', 'the best in the world' or 'always out in front'.
- Sometimes the aim of a business will be contained in its **mission statement** or vision.
- The main aim for a start-up business is survival; further aims may be profit, growth or bigger market share.
- Most businesses will aim to satisfy their customers.
- Owners may also want to achieve other aims, such as independence, a good reputation and loyal customers.
- Businesses often have aims to act ethically and sustainably.

Fotolia

A football club can measure its progress by its position in the league

- Acting ethically means doing the right thing or being moral: for example, not using child labour or exploiting poorer countries.
- Acting sustainably is an environmental aim that means that the business should take no more out of the environment than it puts back in.
- This is achieved through green energy, recycling, creating less waste and using sustainable resources.
- The steps on the way to achieving an aim will be marked by shorter-term objectives.
- Objectives will be more clearly defined than aims — setting them helps the business move forward.
- Progress can be measured by seeing how well objectives have been met.
- 'SMART' is the term used to remember what objectives should be in order to be useful to a business.
- SMART objectives are Specific, Measurable, Achievable, Realistic and Time-related.

Speak the language

aims — long-term goals towards which a business can work

ethical aims and objectives — aiming to 'do the right thing'

mission statement — a statement of the values and ambitions of a business that defines how it operates

objectives — shorter-term targets that can be measured

sustainable aims and objectives — aiming to be environmentally friendly

In a nutshell

* Aims are long-term 'wishes'.
* Objectives are shorter term and more precise.
* The main aim of a start-up business will be survival.
* Further aims include profit, growth and bigger market share.
* Some aims involve ethics and the environment.
* Objectives can be used to help manage a business and measure its progress.

Test yourself

Try this exam-style question.

Rachel has started a business called Kidzstuff selling children's clothes. She designs and makes the clothes herself. She has decided to rent a shop in her village for 6 months to build up trade.

1 State a suitable aim for Kidzstuff. *(1 mark)*

2 Explain why this is a relevant aim for Rachel's business. *(2 marks)*

3 Explain how Rachel could use objectives to help reach her aim. *(2 marks)*

Boost *your grade*

AO1 to AO2: to reach AO2 marks you may need to explain the difference between aims and objectives. You may need to give relevant examples from the business that you are given. Always put your answer in the context of this business.

Topic 4
The influence of stakeholders

What the specification requires

You need to know what is meant by the term **stakeholder** in connection with business. You need to understand that stakeholders can both be influenced by the actions of a business, and also have an influence on the actions of a business. In particular, you should understand how stakeholders can influence small businesses.

In brief

Businesses can only exist if people take risks on new products or new ideas or in new markets. The owners of the business are usually the ones who carry most of the risk. They obviously have a stake in how well the business succeeds. Once a business does exist, it has many people, other than the owners, who have an interest in its success (or failure). Stakeholders are those people, groups or organisations that have a stake in a business.

Employees are internal stakeholders

Revision notes

- Stakeholders with a direct interest in the business are called **internal stakeholders** and include owners and employees. In a small business, the owners will be a single person (sole trader), or a small group of people (partnerships, co-operatives, private limited companies).
- **Shareholders** are a special group of owners. Each has a share of the business. In private limited companies, shareholders are limited to family and friends.
- Owners would like success and profit. They can influence a business by investing. Owners make key decisions about the business, such as what to sell, what markets to operate in and whether to expand.

- Employees would like decent working conditions and fair pay. Employees can influence the business through working hard and being skilled and motivated — or not.
- Managers are the employees who help run the business. Their influence extends to taking day-to-day decisions in the business.
- **External stakeholders** have a less direct stake in a business. They include customers, suppliers, banks, communities, government and pressure groups.
- Customers want quality and reliability. They influence the business by buying or not.

- Suppliers influence the business through quality and reliability of supply.
- Financial stakeholders, such as banks, have lent or given the business money. They can take decisions that are in their own interests, rather than those of the business.
- The community may want the business for some reasons (employment) but not others (pollution).
- Government influences business through laws and taxation.
- Pressure groups try to influence businesses to bring about change.

Speak the language

external stakeholders — individuals, groups or other businesses that have a less direct interest in a business

internal stakeholders — those with a direct interest in a business

shareholders — owners of shares in a business (all shareholders are stakeholders but not vice versa)

stakeholder — a person, group or organisation with an interest in a business

In a nutshell

* All businesses have stakeholders.
* Internal stakeholders have a direct stake.
* They can influence the business through the way they work and make decisions.
* External stakeholders have a more indirect stake.
* They can have a lot of influence on a small business, however, e.g. customers not buying, suppliers not providing quality, governments setting tax too high.

Boost your grade

AO2 to AO3: sometimes stakeholder groups have conflicting aims. For example, customers may want lower prices while shareholders want higher profits; suppliers may want paying immediately while the business wants to delay payment; a business may want to expand operations, while the community wants to keep it small. AO3-level marks will be indicated by the key words 'analyse' or 'evaluate'. This means you must look at both sides of an argument with equal weight. You may then be asked to make a decision (e.g. should the business expand or not). There is no right or wrong answer. AO3 marks are gained for the reasons you give for your judgement.

Test yourself

Try this exam-style question.

Angie owns a drive-in burger bar. It normally shuts at 10 p.m. As the local cinema has decided to stay open until midnight, Angie has decided to extend her opening hours. She is in a residential district and local people have complained about late-night traffic noise. They have appealed to the local council to restrict the burger bar to 10 p.m. closing.

Fotolia

1 Identify two stakeholders in this situation. *(2 marks)*

2 Select two stakeholders and explain how their aims conflict. *(3 marks)*

3 Advise the council whether or not to uphold the appeal. *(7 marks)*

Topic 5
Business planning to reduce risk

What the specification requires

You need to understand that, to be effective, a business needs to plan. In particular, planning helps the business when it is setting up and raising finance. You will need to know the main sections of a **business plan** and why they are important. You should be clear about how a business plan can be used to reduce the risks of failure. You will not be expected, or asked, to write a business plan.

In brief

The business plan is an outline of the aims and objectives the business intends to achieve. It describes the methods, staff and products it intends to use to try to achieve them. It should include financial details and forecasts. Ideally, it should be based on **market research** into the business's chosen market. It should include all aspects of the business, not just finance but the products for sale and the **marketing strategy**, structure and administration of the business. It is often used as a tool for raising finance.

Revision notes

- A good business plan lays down the direction that the business will take and outlines aims and objectives for the first couple of years.
- It is both a working document for the business and an important management tool that should be updated at regular intervals.
- New businesses often need loans from banks to help them start. A business plan is a useful tool to help gain a loan.
- The main sections of a typical business plan include:
  - a brief introduction to the business, saying what it sells and how it will stand out from the competition, including its aims and objectives
  - the USP of the business — its **unique selling point**
  - details of the owners' qualifications and experience

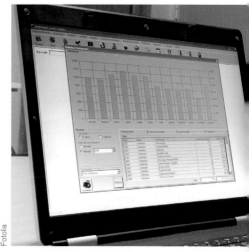

Fotolia

Plans kept electronically can easily be updated

- details of the market in which the business hopes to operate
- the legal format of the business
- basic costings for the product and a forecast of where the business expects to break even
- market information drawn from market research to show the target market and how it will be reached
- the current financial position of the business and how it intends to raise any further money
- any other factors of note — these should include any information that has not been covered elsewhere in the plan but is relevant to the success of the business

Speak the language

business plan — a detailed description and forecast for a business, used to reduce risk

market research — details found out about the business's chosen market

marketing strategy — the ways in which the business intends to promote and sell its product

unique selling point — the factor that makes the business or product a 'one-off'

■ New businesses are at risk of failure. Risks include lack of demand for a product, costs that are too high, competition, staff who are not experienced, and not enough detailed knowledge of the market.

■ All of these risks can be reduced through a good business plan.

In a nutshell

* New businesses often start with a lot of risks.
* A business plan helps reduce these risks.
* It can be used to help raise finance and support.
* It is also a tool to help manage the progress of the business.

Boost your grade

AO1 to AO2: AO1 marks will often be gained from questions asking you to 'give' or 'describe', e.g. 'Give two reasons why Fred should write a business plan.' AO2 marks will be for 'explain', e.g. 'Explain which reason is more important to Fred.'

Test yourself

Fill in the missing words using the list below. If you are feeling confident, cover the words and do the exercise from memory.

Many .... businesses face the risk of .... A business plan outlines the aims and .... of a business. It helps the business to see where its .... and weaknesses lie. It should be based on .... into the business's chosen market. It should include ...., ... and .... details. It is often used to help raise .... by being presented to a .... or other lending institution.

bank   finance   financial   market   market research
objectives   product   start-up   failure   strengths

Choosing a legal structure

What the specification requires

You should know and understand that a small business, especially a start-up business, is limited to certain types of legal organisation. These are **sole trader**, **partnership** and **private limited company**. You need to know what is meant by **limited liability** and how this can be of benefit to a business. You also need to understand how increasing the number of stakeholders can bring both advantages and disadvantages.

In brief

Only certain types of legal structure are appropriate for a small business. The smallest is the 'one person' business called the sole trader. Partnerships are agreements between two or more people to share the responsibilities and organisation of the

Partnerships draw on the expertise and resources of more than one person

business — and also to share the workload and profits (or losses). Both of these have the drawback of unlimited **liability** for the owners. Private limited companies bring the owners the benefit of limiting their liability, but could also bring them problems by introducing more stakeholders, with different aims and objectives for the business.

Revision notes

- A start-up business will probably be a sole trader, partnership or private limited company.
- A sole trader is a business that is owned and run by one person.
- The owner raises the finance him- or herself, from personal sources (own funds) or by borrowing. The owner has sole control of the business, makes all the decisions and receives any profit.
- Sole traders gain from being independent.

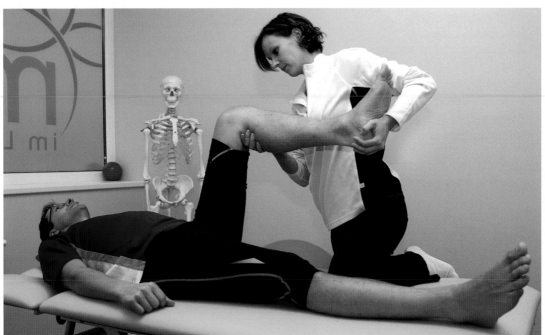

A freelance physiotherapist is an example of a sole trader

- Raising more money is often hard, so expanding the business may be difficult.
- A partnership is a business that is owned by two or more people jointly. Partnerships benefit from shared responsibility and extra expertise. Partners may disagree and this can harm the business. Owners raise the finance themselves, from personal sources or by borrowing. The joint owners receive any profit and share risk equally unless a Deed of Partnership states otherwise.
- In sole traders and partnerships, owners are personally responsible for all the debts of the business. Sole traders and partnerships are easy and cheap to set up; no formal paperwork is needed.
- Sole traders and partnerships each have unlimited liability. The owners are responsible for the debts of the business up to the whole extent that they are able to pay. Liability means the responsibility of the owner for the debts of the business. It is possible to limit this.
- Private limited companies have limited liability. This can be of benefit to the business's reputation, but banks may be reluctant to lend to small companies, without guarantees.
- Private companies have to be legally established and registered at Companies House. They must produce certain accounts, which are available to the public.
- Extra stakeholders, such as shareholders, can mean disagreements.

Speak the language

liability — the responsibility of the owner for the debts of the business

limited liability — when liability is limited to the amount a shareholder has invested

partnership — a business with unlimited liability owned and run by two or more people

private limited company — a business with shareholders that has limited liability

sole trader — a business with unlimited liability owned and run by one person

In a nutshell

* Start-up businesses will be organised as sole traders, partnerships or private limited companies.
* Each legal type is suitable for a small business.
* Sole traders carry all the responsibility themselves, but gain all of any profit.
* Partners share both responsibility and profit.
* Private companies protect themselves by limiting their liability.

Test yourself

Try this exam-style question.

George is an accountant, Harry is a chef. George and Harry wish to set up a catering business as a partnership. Explain two benefits to them of setting up as a partnership.

(4 marks)

Boost your grade

AO1 to AO2: you will need to provide explanations and examples to move from AO1 to AO2. AO1 is usually 'give' or describe'. Always put your answer in context, using information from the case study, to gain AO2 marks.

Topic 7
Choosing a location

What the specification requires

Businesses need to take a number of key decisions when setting up. You will need to learn about and understand the factors that influence the choice of a start-up business location. These include **start-up costs**; how easy it is to access both raw materials and the intended market; whether or not transport, labour and the right technology are all available; and likely levels of competition.

In brief

Businesses need to decide not only what they are going to sell, but also from where they are going to sell it. One of the most important decisions that an **entrepreneur** has to make is where the business will be based. Several factors may influence this. For some businesses a single factor will stand out, for others a combination of factors will be important. For many, the nature of the good or service they are selling is key. All businesses, even the smallest online ones, need to have somewhere from which to trade.

Revision notes

- There are many factors that influence location.
- The ideal location will not be too expensive, but will help the business to attract customers.
- There are government grants and other packages of assistance to help businesses set up in certain areas. The EU also provides regional assistance.
- Some businesses can only be located near to certain natural factors that are essential to them. The most obvious of these are those businesses dealing in extracting raw materials.

Roberto Burgos S. Costa Rica

Location may not be a matter of choice

- Customers may need to visit a shop or other **retail outlet**. Such outlets need display and storage space along with parking or public transport for customers.
- Internet shopping lets customers view stock and buy online, so some businesses have done away with other retail outlets.
- Service providers (like plumbers and hairdressers) must be close to their markets.
- Good transport or **infrastructure** links are vital for both suppliers and customers. Suppliers need access to bring materials in; customers need to be able to reach the business.
- In some cases, a business may need a large workforce, or may need a workforce with particular qualifications, skills or specialisms.
- Having competitors close by can bring benefits to a business, as people 'shop around'. It can also make it easier to work with suppliers. However, in other cases, businesses will need to locate away from competitors.
- In modern businesses, new technology for communications is vital (such as a broadband connection). Businesses may also need specialist machinery.

Dell only sells online

In a nutshell

All businesses must operate from somewhere, even if it is only the spare bedroom! Where they operate from depends on the nature of the product, process or service they are selling. For a new business, factors influencing location include:
* cost, including any national and international government assistance
* availability of raw materials
* location and ease of access for customers
* location and ease of access for suppliers
* location and skills of workers
* location and strength of competition
* availability of the right technology

Boost your grade **AO2 to AO3:** to reach AO3 marks you must show that you can analyse (weigh up both sides of an argument) and judge (come to a decision). There is not always a right or wrong answer so, when asked to compare two locations for a business, you should weigh up the good and bad points of each, make a decision, and say why you have made it (justification). To gain top marks, this must be done using the business you have been given.

Test yourself

Choose the correct answer from the following alternatives.

1 The costs a business pays once, when it is first established, are called: **(a)** start-up costs, **(b)** set-up costs, **(c)** beginning costs, **(d)** establishment costs.

2 Its location may depend on whether it sells goods or **(a)** clothes, **(b)** food, **(c)** services, **(d)** products.

3 A business extracting raw materials will be located: **(a)** on the high street, **(b)** near customers, **(c)** near technology, **(d)** near raw materials.

4 Service providers need to locate close to **(a)** shops, **(b)** markets, **(c)** raw materials, **(d)** technology.

5 National and international help for new businesses can help keep down **(a)** revenue, **(b)** costs, **(c)** customers, **(d)** taxes.

Section test: Starting a business

Read Item A and then answer the questions that follow.

Item A

Marie and Mark have discovered that many people do not bother to print photographs any more, but store them electronically. They found that, with their own photographs, they could not remember what was in a particular file, as the photographs were not named. The easiest way to remember where photographs were was to print off a single sheet of thumbnails of the photographs.

The two friends think they have found a gap in the market. They have decided to set up a business that provides thumbnails on a card that is the right size to fit into a CD or DVD casing. Customers forward their photographs, and Marie and Mark make the thumbnail card and return it.

Questions

1 (a) What is meant by a 'gap in the market'? *(1 mark)*
   (b) Give two reasons why Mark and Marie should write a business plan. *(4 marks)*

2 Mark and Marie are going to use Mark's computer but still face certain start-up costs. These include:
- buying the software to make the thumbnails
- advertising the service

   Explain which cost you think is most important, and why. *(6 marks)*

3 Mark thinks the business should be set up as a partnership, but Marie thinks it should be a private limited company. Compare the two forms of ownership and advise the friends which would be more suitable. Give reasons for your judgement. *(9 marks)*

Total: 20 marks

Topic 8

Conducting market research within limited budgets

What the specification requires

Market research is an important and very large field in business. However, many methods of market research are either too expensive or too difficult for a small business to carry out. You should therefore limit yourself to learning about those types of market research that might be suitable for a small business, on a limited budget.

In brief

Businesses need to collect information to help them to sell products to their customers. They need to know which group of customers might buy the product, how much they might be willing to spend, how often they will buy and what is attracting them to the product — why do they want to buy. They can find out this information through various means, such as asking questions or looking at market data. With this information the business can decide not only what to sell, but also how to change a product or develop new products to attract customers.

Revision notes

- The two most common ways to divide market research is into **desk research** and **field research**. Field research is also called primary research. It means that data are being collected for the first time.
- Field research makes sure that the **data** collected are exactly what is needed and are up to date. However, it can be expensive and time consuming.
- It is often carried out using questionnaires — lists of questions asked of a target audience. It also uses surveys to collect information: for example, on buying habits. In retail outlets, till roll information may be available for this. Surveys can also be carried out by telephone.
- Businesses can observe how customers behave. They can also ask for feedback from customers and suppliers.

- Focus groups are small groups asked for their opinions. A specialist type of focus group is a tasting or testing group who try the product and give feedback.
- Desk research is also called secondary research. It uses data and information that have already been collected.
- Desk research can be cheap or even free but it does not necessarily provide exactly the information needed. It can also be expensive to obtain particular information, and it quickly goes out of date and may be unreliable. For instance, the business may be relying on someone else's interpretation of data.
- The main sources for desk research are books, newspapers, magazines, journals and other publications, such as reports. Company reports are free and easily obtained; many market reports are expensive, so they would not be appropriate to small businesses.
- The internet is a secondary source. Information is often free, but it is not always reliable.

Desk and field research compared

	Advantages	Disadvantages
Field research	■ Up to date ■ Targeted	■ Expensive ■ Time consuming ■ Large surveys needed for accuracy
Desk research	■ Cheap, even free ■ Easy to obtain	■ Out of date ■ Not exactly what is wanted ■ Some can be expensive

Fotolia

Desk research is cheap but it may be out of date

In a nutshell

* Only certain types of market research are appropriate to smaller businesses.
* The main types are field (primary) research and desk (secondary) research.
* Field research is more reliable, but time consuming and expensive.
* Desk research is cheap — often free — but may be out of date or unreliable.

Test yourself

Choose the correct answer from the following alternatives.

1 Market research is usually divided into desk research and **(a)** open research, **(b)** field research, **(c)** closed research, **(d)** concentrated research.

2 The two main types of research are known as **(a)** primary and tertiary, **(b)** secondary and tertiary, **(c)** primary and secondary, **(d)** outside and inside.

3 A small group asked for an opinion on a product is called **(a)** a focus group, **(b)** a delta group, **(c)** observation, **(d)** market data.

4 Company reports can be useful because they are easy to obtain and **(a)** free, **(b)** complicated, **(c)** online, **(d)** expensive.

5 The internet is a source that often provides free information. The main problem with this information is that it is not always **(a)** reliable, **(b)** easy to read, **(c)** searchable, **(d)** in English.

Boost your grade

AO2 to AO3: when presented with market research data, always ask yourself how valid it is. Look at the source and date. If you don't have raw data, but an opinion, this could be less reliable. For AO3 marks, use these arguments to support your analysis of data and as the reasons to support your judgements.

Using the marketing mix: product and price

What the specification requires

Marketing, and the use of the 'four Ps', is part of every business. You should be able to recommend an appropriate mix for a smaller business, with a limited budget. You need to understand what sort of products a small business will offer and how it can alter these to meet its customers' needs. You also need to understand the basic relationship between price and demand.

In brief

There are four key areas used to market any product. These are the four parts of the 'marketing mix'. Price, product, promotion and place are often just known as the 'four Ps'.

Fotolia

Goods can be touched and felt

It is important to remember that each part is just one-quarter of the marketing mix, and that it is important for a business to get the balance right. It is no use having a fantastic product if no one knows about it, or if it can only be made at a price that no one is willing to pay.

Revision notes

- The **product** is the result of business activity. Without a product the business has nothing to sell. Products can be either goods or services. Goods can be touched and felt; services are invisible and are done for or to a person or organisation. Examples of personal services for individuals and groups are plumbing, entertainment, taxi rides and tourism. Examples of commercial services are insurance, retailing and transport.
- Some businesses sell a variety of products (**product range**); others sell just one. Small businesses that sell a narrow range are vulnerable to market changes. For example, a taxi business selling just taxi rides could be hit by increased car ownership. By making the range

wider (e.g. mini-buses, limousines), a cushion against market change is provided.

- Most small businesses can find out what else customers want, and try to provide it.
- Price is the amount at which a business offers products for sale. Price × sales = **revenue**. A business would like revenue to cover costs (break even). The price of a product may be linked to a number of factors, including its cost, the price of competing products, the level of profit the business wants and the need for quick sales.
- Demand is usually higher at lower prices and vice versa. This means an increase in price is likely to lead to a fall in demand, fewer sales and lower profits. Smaller businesses therefore must be very careful about changing price. This is especially true if there are competing products at competitive prices.

Speak the language

product — the good or service produced for sale

product range — the variety of products on offer from a business

revenue — the income of a business from sales

Fotolia

Entertainment is a kind of service

In a nutshell

* Product and price are two important parts of the marketing mix.
* Product is the good or service for sale.
* Price is the amount at which a business offers the product for sale.
* Increases in price will affect demand, and fewer products will be sold (and vice versa).
* Businesses in competition therefore have to be careful about changing price.

Test yourself

Choose the correct answer from the following alternatives.

1 The product is the result of business **(a)** profits, **(b)** activity, **(c)** demand, **(d)** marketing.

2 A product that can be touched is called **(a)** a good, **(b)** a personal service, **(c)** a commercial service, **(d)** a range.

3 A product that is done to or for someone is called **(a)** a good, **(b)** a range, **(c)** a variety, **(d)** a service.

4 A business selling many products has a wide **(a)** demand, **(b)** price range, **(c)** product range, **(d)** number of customers.

5 A narrow product range leaves a business vulnerable to **(a)** low prices, **(b)** taxation, **(c)** changes in the product, **(d)** changes in the market.

6 Breakeven is when total revenue is equal to total **(a)** profit, **(b)** price, **(c)** sales, **(d)** cost.

7 Total revenue is calculated as price times **(a)** profit, **(b)** price, **(c)** sales, **(d)** cost.

8 If prices fall, demand tends to **(a)** fall, **(b)** rise, **(c)** stay the same, **(d)** be worth more.

9 A business that increases prices could see a fall in all the following *except* **(a)** revenue, **(b)** profit, **(c)** demand, **(d)** product range.

10 Customers are more likely to move their business if there are **(a)** competitors, **(b)** suppliers, **(c)** more customers, **(d)** no price changes.

AO1: to access AO1 marks, you need to show that you have relevant knowledge. When using terms like 'product', therefore, you should always provide a definition and, if you can think of one, an example.

Topic 10
Using the marketing mix: promotion and place

What the specification requires

You need to understand that, although promotion is vital to business success, only certain promotions are suitable for small businesses on a limited budget. You should therefore be able to recommend appropriate types of promotion. When learning about place in the marketing mix, you need to understand the growing importance of e-commerce.

In brief

Promotion refers to the methods that a business uses to communicate to consumers, first, that its product exists and, second, that it has features that a consumer will like. Promotion is therefore used to inform customers and to try to persuade them to buy.

Place refers both to the place where a product is sold and to how the product gets to that place. This includes any 'place' from where a customer can buy a good or service, not just shops, but also 'virtual' places such as the internet. The second part is **distribution**. It is how the product gets to the customer.

TopFoto

Businesses can promote their goods at industry trade fairs

Revision notes

- Promotion consists of telling customers that a product exists and persuading them to buy it. Advertising is publicity for a product that is paid for directly, called **above-the-line** expenditure.
- Advertising is used to promote products through broadcast and print media such as television, radio, posters, magazines, leaflets and point-of-sale material. For a small business, the most useful advertising is through local newspapers. Only certain types of advertising are suitable. Television and billboard advertising, for example, would not be appropriate or affordable.

Transport at each stage of the chain adds to costs

- **Below-the-line** expenditure is promotion other than direct advertising. It is not paid for directly.
- In promoting a product, a small business may use money-off coupons, free samples and special offers. Other promotions that may be effective include the use of flyers and leaflets, printed stationery and business cards. Businesses can also sponsor local events or teams.
- Personal endorsements, i.e. 'word of mouth' recommendation, are vital to small businesses.
- Retailers can use promotions like 'buy one, get one free', and promotional price reductions, but they have to be careful about how much they cost.
- Place covers both where a product can be bought and how it gets to that place.
- Finding the right place and distribution channels depends on the target market.
- **E-commerce** has opened up much wider markets so that some products (such as music tracks) can now easily be distributed online. Small businesses can offer internet sales with an online ordering service backed up by home delivery using couriers or the postal service.

In a nutshell

* Promotion tells consumers about products and tries to sell them.
* Promotion is advertising and other promotions.
* Small businesses can advertise locally through newspapers and leaflets.
* Small businesses can use some promotions, such as sponsorship, but must keep an eye on their budgets.
* Place refers to where a customer buys and delivery to that place.
* E-commerce has extended the market for small businesses.

Boost your grade

AO1 to AO2: one way to boost your grade from AO1 to AO2 is to provide explanations. For example, you should be able to explain why a national television promotion campaign would be unsuitable for a small business. Key words like 'because' and 'as' show that you are explaining reasons.

Test yourself

Match the term on the left with the correct phrase on the right.

1 'above-the-line' expenditure

2 'below-the-line' expenditure

3 broadcast and print media

4 distribution

5 e-commerce

6 personal endorsements

7 place

8 promotion

to inform and persuade customers

where a product is sold

how the product gets to the customer

publicity for a product that is paid for directly

publicity for a product that is not paid for directly

buying and selling online

'word-of-mouth' recommendation

television, radio, posters and magazines

Section test: Marketing

Read Item A and then answer the questions that follow.

Item A

Abby has decided to start a business making personalised birthday and other greetings cards for people. She thinks that there is a gap in the market, as she has made cards for many of her friends, and they have all commented on how good they were.

She faces competition from a local newsagent that sells cards, and also the post office.

Questions

1 Explain TWO reasons why it would be advisable for Abby to undertake
  market research. *(5 marks)*

2 Suggest and justify an appropriate method of market research for
  this business. *(6 marks)*

Read Item B and then answer question 3.

Item B

Abby's sales are going well, but a local supermarket is now planning to sell a range of 'handmade' cards.

3 Discuss how Abby might respond to this competition. *(9 marks)*

Total: 20 marks

Topic 11
Finance and support for a small business

What the specification requires

You need to learn about the organisations that support new businesses, and the advice and support that is available. You should be aware that small businesses do not always find it easy to raise finance. You should learn about the different sources of finance available to a small business, and be able to say when each would be appropriate.

In brief

The money which a business needs may come from its owners, from lenders or people who are willing to take a risk, or from other outside sources. Small businesses will usually start with the owners' own funds as capital. They may also have some inputs from friends and family. Outside of this, it is usual to borrow money. Because small businesses might struggle, there are both government and charitable organisations that will help them.

Revision notes

- Small businesses may have difficulty raising the finance that they need.
- **Owners' funds** are one of the main sources of finance. It is the money that the owners already have. Limited companies can raise funds by selling shares to the owners (the shareholders). Owners may also raise finance from friends and family or from private investors called **venture capitalists**.
- A business may keep some profit for future finance. This is called **retained profit**.
- If business owners do not already have the funds, they will borrow.

Fotolia

Every business needs money

The most common forms of business borrowing are:

- trade credit — when a business promises to pay later for goods received now (hopefully, after it has sold them)
- **overdraft** — a bank allows the business to take more out of its account than it has deposited, up to an agreed limit; this is flexible and interest is only charged on what is actually owed
- loans — a business borrows a fixed amount, for a fixed term, with regular repayments made and interest charged on the full amount for the term of the loan
- hire purchase — paying a deposit and buying in instalments (e.g. a vehicle or machine)
- leasing — effectively, renting vehicles, equipment and plant
- mortgages — long-term loans used to buy expensive items such as land or buildings, secured on the item bought

- ■ Business support is available from organisations such as the government through the Business Start Up Scheme and charities like the Prince's Trust.
- ■ The government encourages banks to lend, and guarantees some small business loans.

Types of borrowing

Short term (from a few days up to 3 years)	Medium term (from 3 years to 10 years)	Long term (10 years +)
■ Overdrafts	■ Hire purchase	■ Loans
■ Loans	■ Loans	■ Mortgages
■ Trade credit	■ Debentures	

Nationwide

Businesses commonly raise finance from banks

In a nutshell

* Small businesses are often started with owners' funds.
* Other private sources of finance are also common.
* Otherwise, businesses will borrow from banks.
* The main forms of borrowing are overdrafts and loans.
* Government and charitable bodies provide support to business.

Boost your grade

AO1: to access AO1 marks for knowledge, you must make sure that your knowledge is relevant. Although venture capitalists are often in the news, they tend to back larger businesses, rather than small start-ups, so before using them as an example, check that they make sense in the context of the business you are given.

Test yourself

Fill in the missing words using the list below. If you are feeling confident, cover the words and do the exercise from memory.

The money which a business needs often comes from its .... This is called .... Other finance will be raised from lenders such as .... It may also come from profits kept back or .... Sometimes people with .... are willing to take a risk on a business. These are called .... Small businesses may also have .... from friends and family. Because small businesses might struggle, there are both .... and charitable organisations that will help them. These include the .... and charities like ....

banks   Business Start Up Scheme   capital   finance   government

owners   owners' funds   retained   the Prince's Trust   venture capitalists

Topic 12
Understanding financial terms

What the specification requires

You need to understand, and apply in the context of a case study, terms such as price, sales, revenue, costs and profit. You will need to use these terms correctly in your answers.

In brief

Businesses produce either a good or a service for sale. If it is a good, there will be raw materials and other inputs to pay for. If it is a service, at the very least the business will need to let people know that it exists. In either case, therefore, there are costs. The money that the business receives for its sales is called **revenue**. Business costs are divided into **fixed costs**, also called indirect costs or overheads, and **variable costs**.

Revision notes

- In the production of goods, or the provision of services, there are costs.
- From the sales of goods or services, businesses make revenue. Price is the amount of money at which a product is offered for sale by a business.
- When total revenue is greater than total cost, the business is making a **profit**. When total revenue is less than total cost, the business is making a **loss**. The point where the amount of total revenue is equal to the amount of total costs is called the **breakeven** point. At this point, the business is making neither a profit nor a loss.
- New businesses face 'start-up' costs that are paid once, when the business begins (e.g. the purchase of a computer for an internet business). These are also called 'sunk' costs.

A till receipt is a familiar financial document

- Costs that have to be continually paid to keep the business operating are called running, or operating, costs. These may be fixed costs such as rent, or variable costs such as wages.
- Costs may be fixed or variable. Total cost is fixed cost plus variable cost. Fixed costs do not vary with output. Examples are rent, interest payments and rates. They are paid whether or not a business is producing. Variable costs vary directly with output. Examples are raw materials, packaging, parts and components, ingredients and power.
- Semi-variable costs vary with output, but not directly. For example, a business may need to pay overtime, or a shop may need to stay open for longer hours.

In a nutshell

* Businesses produce goods or services for sale at a price.
* Sales at that price produce revenue.
* If revenue is greater than cost, the business is in profit.
* If cost is greater than revenue, the business is making a loss.
* Costs can be listed in many different ways.

Test yourself

Try this exam-style question.

Alberus plc is a well-known chain of high-street shops, selling a range of goods, including clothes, food and household goods. The business also sells services such as insurance and has its own credit card and bank.

Alberus has a number of different revenue sources. It also has different costs.

1 Describe one fixed and one variable cost. *(2 marks)*

2 Describe three possible major revenue sources. *(3 marks)*

3 Explain which revenue source is most important to the business and why. *(5 marks)*

Boost *your grade*

AO1 to AO2: to access AO2 marks, you must explain your answers in context. This means that you should make every effort to use the business in the case study, and refer to the products it sells.

Topic 13
Calculating profit and loss

What the specification requires

You will need to be able to make simple calculations to work out amounts in a business. For example, you should be able to calculate revenue from price and sales information, and outcomes such as profit or loss from revenue and cost information.

In brief

To know how well a business is doing, it is necessary to calculate all of its costs and revenues. The difference between the two totals will tell you whether the business is making a profit or not. It is important to include *all* costs and revenues. Sometimes the cost of the owners' own time is not included and this gives a false picture of profitability.

Revision notes

- Revenue is the income of the business. It is usually calculated as the number of products sold × the price of each product (good or service).
- Different products have different types of price. **Rent** is the price to use land or property. **Wages and salaries** are the price of somebody's labour. Interest is the price of borrowing.
- Calculations of profit and loss are usually shown on a profit and loss account. Profit is said to be the reward for enterprise, or risk taking.
- **Gross profit** is calculated by taking the cost of sales (i.e. the cost of inputs such as raw materials, or parts, or stock) from total revenue. **Net profit** is calculated by then taking off **expenses** — running or operating costs (also called overheads) such as power, labour, fuel, communications, loan interest, rent and rates.
- In a small business, it is important to make sure all costs (such as the sole trader's time, for example) have been included in the calculations.

Speak the language

expenses — the day-to-day running costs of the business (also called overheads or operating costs)

gross profit — total revenue minus cost of sales

net profit — gross profit minus expenses (also called overheads or operating profit)

rent — the price for land or buildings

wages and salaries — the price for labour

- Breakeven is where total costs are equal to total revenue, i.e. there is neither profit nor loss.
- Breakeven charts and graphs can be used to predict where a profit will be made, and can help the business to plan.

In a nutshell

revenue = price × number sold

revenue − cost = profit (if positive), loss (if negative)

gross profit = revenue − cost of sales

net profit = gross profit − overheads

It is essential to make sure all costs are included.

Boost your grade

AO1 to AO2: when given examples of accounts such as profit and loss accounts, AO1 marks are given usually for knowing how to work out various figures — such as net profit — while AO2 marks are given for analysing the figures. So you should be asking not just 'is this a good net profit?' but 'is it good for this type of business?'

Test yourself

Try this exam-style question.

Furness Ltd is a worldwide business, specialising in the manufacture and sale of sports equipment, sports clothing and sports shoes. Some financial figures for Furness are provided in the table.

Trading account (part)	2006	2005	2004
Turnover (sales revenue) (£m)	5,000	4,800	4,550
Trading (operating) profit (£m)	900	750	710
Retained profit (£m)	220	200	180
Trading profit margin (£m)	18.00%	15.62%	?
Marketing expenditure (£m)	1,000	900	750

1 Calculate the percentage increase in retained profit between 2005 and 2006. *(3 marks)*

2 Describe what other factors, apart from the level of operating profit, could influence the amount of retained profit kept by Furness. *(6 marks)*

Section test: Finance

Read Item A and then answer the questions that follow.

Item A

John and Jackson have seen the growth in hand car wash businesses in their local area. They think that they can provide a better service that combines the efficiency of a machine car wash with the personal service of a hand car wash. They have rented a site by a busy main road, where they intend to install a machine. There is an existing building where they will put a comfortable waiting area for customers. Here customers can buy coffee, watch television and buy car care products. Cars will be cleaned inside, washed in the machine, and then finished with hand polishing.

1 Outline the main costs and revenues for the business. *(4 marks)*

2 Explain two methods that John and Jackson might have used to finance their business start-up. *(4 marks)*

3 The car wash machine will cost around £15,000. John and Jackson have left themselves the choice of:
   (a) borrowing £15,000 from Jackson's father, for which he would want a shareholding
   (b) borrowing £15,000 in a 5-year bank loan, secured on the machine

Discuss the advantages and disadvantages of each possible source. Recommend which would be the best option.
Give reasons for your answer. *(12 marks)*

Total: 20 marks

Topic 15
Recruitment

What the specification requires

You should understand that businesses need staff and that they recruit staff both from within the business and from outside it. You should know which factors help decide a person's pay. Payment is not always in the form of wages and there may be other, non-monetary, rewards for employees.

In brief

Businesses need both full-time and part-time employees. They will use internal and external methods to recruit them, whichever is more appropriate. They will pay employees according to their qualities, such as skill and experience. Employees will also gain other benefits, such as pensions and bonuses. Not all benefits will be in the form of money; some non-monetary rewards may also be available in some businesses.

Revision notes

- **Recruitment** is the process by which a business finds new employees. There are a number of reasons why a business might need new staff: the business could be growing, employees may have left or retired, or new skills may be needed. The business may need full- or part-time employees.
- Even a small business, such as a sole trader, may need to recruit employees.
- The business has to decide whether to recruit from outside the business (**external**) or from its existing employees (**internal**). Recruiting internally is often cheaper, however recruiting externally brings in new people and ideas.
- Methods include recommendation, advertising and interviewing. The selection process usually starts with an advertisement. Applicants' **CVs** and letters of support are read. Short-listed applicants

Retirement creates a need for recruitment

are invited to interview. Interviews could be one to one, or in front of a panel. The interview might even involve tests to see whether the candidate can really do the job. After the interviews, the best candidate is offered the job. If the candidate accepts, he or she is then appointed.

- Employees with better skills or experience, or more appropriate qualifications for the job, will be paid at a higher rate.
- Many businesses provide other monetary benefits as well as pay, such as pension schemes, bonuses or profit sharing.
- Employees may also be entitled to non-monetary benefits. Many will be linked to the market in which the business operates, such as subsidised travel at a holiday business, cheap loans at a bank, and discounts for retail staff.

Speak the language

CV — curriculum vitae: an applicant's record of their skills, experience and qualifications

external recruitment — recruiting from outside the business

internal recruitment — recruiting from inside the business

recruitment — the process of selecting and employing staff

In a nutshell

* Even the smallest businesses may need employees.
* Recruitment may be a formal process from job advertisement through interview to appointment.
* The recruitment process can also be informal (e.g. by recommendation).
* Some posts may be filled through internal recruitment, some by external recruitment. Each has benefits and drawbacks.

Boost your grade

AO1: AO1 marks are given for the correct use of terms and concepts, so, for instance, you should be able to describe what is meant by 'internal' and 'external' recruitment methods and use these terms.

Test yourself

Fill in the missing words using the list below to complete the recruitment process. If you are feeling confident, cover the words and do the exercise from memory.

The business will write a .... to show what tasks, skills and qualifications are needed and a .... to show the sort of worker that will fit the requirements. It .... the post and invites .... Using letters and .... that are sent in, it draws up a .... of the .... it thinks are best qualified. These become .... and are invited to .... The successful .... is offered the job.

advertises   applicants   applications   candidates   CVs   interview
interviewee   job description   person specification   short-list

Topic 16
Motivating staff

What the specification requires

You should understand that businesses gain if their employees are keen to work hard, and you should be able to suggest suitable and relevant ways for a small business to motivate its employees. You will not be asked to explain any of the theories of motivation.

In brief

Motivation means persuading an employee to work because they want to, generally because they can see a benefit from the action. In a business, a motivated worker will work harder, better and more effectively. Sometimes a word of praise or congratulation is enough to motivate; sometimes it needs to be something more solid. In the case of a small business, the motivation for owners may be to show that they can be a success, or be independent.

Revision notes

- All businesses benefit from having owners and employees who are well motivated. Motivation means people working more effectively because they want to, usually because they may win some sort of reward.
- Businesses use a variety of ways to motivate workers. Some may be financial, such as bonuses or profit sharing. They may also offer non-financial benefits that may be more psychological, such as praise and promotion to a higher status.
- Different people can be motivated in different ways, depending on their outlook and aims. A business must decide which are the most suitable methods of motivation for its situation.
- Small businesses may offer motivation linked to their market segment. For example, a retail outlet could offer a reward for extra sales, or a prize for the most successful salesperson. A service outlet

Praise or reward is often a good way to motivate

could reward employees on the basis of customer feedback, with prizes such as 'employee of the month' and rewards to go with this.

- Small businesses may also be able to motivate employees by helping them to further their careers: for example, by providing or supporting them in training or education.
- Higher status can be used to motivate — giving someone more responsibility, or a more important job title, may help them to be more effective.

Speak the language

motivation — when someone works harder because they want to

In a nutshell

* Motivated workers are better and more efficient at their jobs.
* They are therefore a greater asset to a business.
* Businesses use a variety of ways to motivate.
* Some involve financial reward (e.g. bonuses).
* Some involve non-financial reward (e.g. praise).

Test yourself

Link the term on the left with the correct term on the right. The terms on the right show ways to motivate or rewards from motivation.

1 financial
2 further a career
3 maximum sales
4 more responsibility
5 non-financial
6 retail outlet
7 service outlet
8 status

status
training
extra sales
customer feedback
profit sharing
promotion
praise
prize

Boost your grade

AO1 to AO2: AO2 analysis marks may be gained by comparing financial and non-financial rewards in terms of cost and effectiveness within the context of the business in the case study.

Topic 17
Protecting staff through understanding legislation

What the specification requires

You need to understand that there are various laws to protect workers and that employers have certain responsibilities to their employees. You should be aware of key legislation in the areas of employment rights, including health and safety, discrimination, equal pay and minimum wages. You will not be asked to quote from specific Acts.

In brief

Employees at a business have certain rights in law. They also have responsibilities. Employers also have rights and responsibilities for their employees. Workers have a right to decent and safe working conditions and fair pay for the work they undertake. Employers have the right to expect employees to be punctual, efficient and loyal, and the responsibility to provide good working conditions and fair pay.

Revision notes

- Basic **employment rights** include the right to safe, healthy and reasonably comfortable working conditions, the right to protection from danger in the workplace, and the right to breaks and holidays. Most of these rights are laid down in employment law, although some are basic human rights — for example, the right for an employee to be treated with courtesy and respect by an employer, and for the employee to treat the employer in the same way.

- Employees, by law, are entitled to a written statement giving rates of pay, terms and conditions of employment, pensions, notice periods and disciplinary procedures.

Health and safety signs have to be clear

- Employees are entitled to join a trade union; to be paid the **minimum wage**; to receive an itemised pay statement; and to receive **redundancy** payments. They must not be unfairly dismissed. Workers also have the right, under EU laws, to take part in the management of the business for which they work.
- The main law regarding health and safety is the Health and Safety at Work Act 1974. This Act ensures that all workers have proper washroom and toilet facilities, ventilation, fire exits and levels of heating and lighting. It also makes employers fit guards to dangerous machines.
- The law states that in all matters of recruitment, selection, training, promotion and other areas of human resources, there should be no **discrimination** on grounds of gender, race, religion, creed, sexual orientation, disability or age. This includes the right to equal pay for equal work or responsibility.

Speak the language

discrimination — acting against someone for a reason they cannot control

employment rights — the rights of workers

minimum wage — the least that, by law, an employer can pay

redundancy — when a person's job is no longer needed

Fotolia

Workers are allowed to join trade unions to fight for their rights

In a nutshell

* Workers are entitled to basic rights from employers.
* Employers also have rights, along with their responsibilities.
* Workers should work in safe, healthy environments.
* They should be paid at least the minimum wage.
* There should be no discrimination in employment.

Test yourself

Choose the correct answer from the following alternatives.

1 One basic employment right is the right to working conditions that **(a)** are safe, **(b)** are convenient, **(c)** have parking, **(d)** are colourful.

2 Workers also have the right to leisure through breaks and **(a)** television, **(b)** holidays, **(c)** gym membership, **(d)** cinema.

3 The main law regarding health and safety is **(a)** the Health and Safety at Work Act 1954, **(b)** the Health and Comfort at Work Act 1974, **(c)** the Health and Safety at Work Act 1974, **(d)** the Healthy Workers Act 1924.

4 The law states that there should be no discrimination on grounds of all of the following *except* **(a)** gender, **(b)** race, **(c)** height, **(d)** age.

5 Employees are entitled to be paid at least **(a)** the going rate, **(b)** the maximum wage, **(c)** the bonus wage, **(d)** the minimum wage.

Boost your grade

AO1: you will not be asked to name specific employment legislation, but it will show good knowledge, for AO1 marks, if you can accurately name the Health and Safety at Work Act 1974 and some of its features.

Section test: People in business

Read Item A and then answer the questions that follow.

Item A

Klondike Sports centre has sporting facilities, a pool and a café area. The manager and his assistant are full time. Personal trainers, pool staff and reception and café staff are part time. All staff receive basic health and safety training. The manager was appointed internally, having been assistant manager.

Part-time staff are paid at minimum wage, although local supermarkets pay at a higher rate. They are often expected to work long hours. Currently there is a shortage of weekend staff and many café staff do not stay in employment for long.

1   Describe what is meant by 'minimum wage'.   *(3 marks)*

2   'The manager was appointed internally'. Describe what this means and explain TWO advantages of this method.   *(5 marks)*

3   Define 'staff turnover'. Explain why turnover for part-time staff is high.   *(5 marks)*

4   Suggest and explain two possible ways to reduce staff turnover. Recommend one way, with reasons.   *(7 marks)*

Total: 20 marks

Topic 18
Methods of production

What the specification requires

You should understand that different methods of production will be used when making a product or providing a service. You should be able to describe job and batch production methods and explain when each would be appropriate. You should also realise that businesses need to operate as efficiently as possible, and new technology may help them to do so.

In brief

Production describes the methods by which raw materials and other inputs are turned into outputs — and eventually into the final product. The method of production will depend on the nature of the product and the nature of the customer. Services are almost always produced to individual standards for individual customers — for example, you can only wear your own haircut! For goods, some will be produced individually, and others in larger amounts and in standard sizes or shapes.

Revision notes

- The main methods of production in small businesses are job and batch.
- **Job production** is where a product is a 'one-off' made to individual specifications: for example, made-to-measure clothes, a fitted kitchen or a customised car. This tends to be the most labour-intensive production method, and can lead to expensive outputs due to the craft skills that are usually needed for such products. Almost all services are individually tailored in this way.

Ingram

Hairdressing is an example of job production, as every customer has individual requirements

- **Batch production** is where the same machinery and labour is used to produce different batches or groups of products. Batch production will take place in any manufacturing process where different sizes or colours are needed. For example, the same dress may be produced in sizes from 8 to 16; the same car in different colours.
- Businesses may be able to lower costs, using changes in technology. For example, computers can help businesses run **just-in-time** systems, where parts, components and other materials arrive just as they are needed.
- A **quality product** is one that does what it is supposed to do. It is one that is, in UK law, 'fit for purpose'. If the product does not do what it should, then the customer has the right to demand a refund. It is therefore vital that businesses make products that are reliable and that consumers will continue to buy.
- A business will set its quality systems to make sure that products are better than the consumer expects. Businesses look at what the law requires and then add to this to please the customer and to beat competition.

Speak the language

batch production — producing different groups of a core product from similar inputs

job production — when just one of a product is produced, using skills

just-in-time — when parts, components etc. only arrive as needed

quality — where a product does what the customer expects it to do

Fotolia

Car manufacture is an example of batch production

In a nutshell

* Production describes how inputs are turned into products.
* Small businesses mostly use job and batch production.
* Job production is used for 'one-off' products.
* Batch production uses the same inputs to make different versions of a product.
* Most services are 'job' produced.
* Businesses can increase efficiency, and lower costs, using new technology.
* Businesses must match the quality that customers require.

Boost your grade

AO1 to AO2: you should be able to explain what is meant by 'quality' and give an example to support your explanation. Use the case study business for your example.

Test yourself

Fill in the missing words using the list below to describe methods of production. If you are feeling confident, cover the words and do the exercise from memory.

Batch production is where the same .... and .... can be used to produce different groups of products. Batch production will take place in any manufacturing process where variations to a basic model are needed, such as different .... or ....

.... is where a product is a 'one-off' made to .... specifications: for example, ..., a fitted kitchen or a customised car. This tends to be the most .... production method, and can lead to .... outputs due to the craft skills that are usually needed for such products. Almost all .... are provided in this way.

colours	expensive	individual	job production	labour
labour-intensive	machinery	made-to-measure clothes	services	sizes

Topic 19
Customer service and the impact of ICT

What the specification requires

You need to understand that the survival and success of small businesses may depend on the quality of their customer service. This should include reliable service, clear product information and good after-sales service. You should know that new technology — especially advances in ICT — has helped to improve customer service. In particular, websites and e-commerce have opened up international markets to customers.

In brief

Customer service is used to attract customers and, more importantly, to keep them. It is much cheaper for a business to retain customers than to try and win new ones. Good customer service is key to a business retaining customers. The most common parts to customer service are providing information and advice, providing after-sales service and providing convenient ways to pay. New technology has opened up new ways to keep customers happy, such as ordering via the internet.

Customers don't like to be kept hanging on

Revision notes

- Good customer service is vital to the success of small businesses.
- A key part of customer service is reliability. For example, shops are expected to be open at the times they state, tradesmen and women to visit when they say, and products to perform to the standards expected of them.
- Information may be given in a number of ways, such as by staff in a retail outlet or call centre, on websites or in material such as catalogues. Packaging also carries information. Information must be accurate and provide, as a minimum, what the law requires — for example, how to use a product safely.

- Advice given about a product must be accurate even if it is verbal. Customers should expect specialist advice if they ask a retail assistant. Staff should be trained to give correct advice.
- **After-sales service** may sometimes be as important as the product. For example, if you bought a car but then found that parts for it were unavailable, the car would be useless. In some cases, after-sales service includes guarantees. Sometimes service extends for years; in other cases, it may involve nothing more than a delivery service, or the wrapping of the product. After-sales service also deals with complaints, refunds and exchanges.
- Businesses offer multiple ways to pay, such as credit, hire purchase, cash, and credit and debit cards, and they provide electronic keypads for transactions.
- Advances in ICT have allowed customer services to develop. Customers can buy and get feedback and advice via the internet. They also have access to a much wider choice of products.

Speak the language

after-sales service — the part of customer service that takes place after a sale is made

customer service — looking after customers to attract and retain them

In a nutshell

* Good customer service is a key factor for small businesses.
* A major part of it is reliability.
* In addition, customer service includes information, advice and after-sales service.
* New technology has increased the range of customer service available.

Test yourself

Customer service can be divided into four parts — information, advice, after-sales and ways to pay. Write down these four parts as headings and, without long back at the revision notes, list the following terms under the appropriate headings.

- accurate
- cards
- clear
- delivery
- packaging
- guarantees
- as required
- cash
- credit
- helpful
- specialist

Boost your grade

AO1 to AO2: for AO2 marks your answer must be in the context of the case study business. For some businesses, different aspects of customer service are going to be more or less important. You should choose the right types to recommend for the business given.

Section test: Operations management

Read Item A and then answer the questions that follow.

Item A

John and Jackson have seen the growth in hand car wash businesses in their local area.
They think that they can provide a better service that combines the efficiency of a machine
car wash with the personal service of a hand car wash. They have rented a site by a busy main
road, where they have installed a machine. Cars are cleaned inside, washed in the machine,
and then finished with hand polishing.

Although offering a quality product, sales are slow. One problem appears to be that their
employees know little about the product on offer and so cannot answer customer questions.

1 Explain what is meant by a 'quality product'.   *(4 marks)*

2 Outline how the law works to prevent consumers being cheated at a
   business such as this.   *(4 marks)*

3 One part of customer service is being able to give advice. Describe the
   other three main parts of customer service.   *(6 marks)*

4 Which of the four areas do you think is the most important in this case
   and how would you solve the problem? Give reasons for your answer.   *(6 marks)*

Total: 20 marks

Practice exam

The paper is marked out of 60 and you have 1 hour in which to complete it. Remember that papers will not cover the whole of the content, but will choose to concentrate on different content each year. The paper has some background information and Items for you to use. Papers will not always be based on a single business.

Background

John and Jackson are two friends who have just left school. They want to set up in business. They have seen the growth in hand car wash businesses in their local area. They think that they can provide a better service that combines the efficiency of a machine car wash with the personal service of a hand car wash.

Item A

John and Jackson are keen to start the business but, before they do so, they have been advised to research the market to find out if their idea might be attractive to customers. They have also been advised that they should set themselves up formally as a business. They are thinking of establishing a partnership as the organisation for the business.

1 (a) **Explain THREE reasons why the friends might want to start a business.** *(6 marks)*

   (b) **Explain TWO methods of market research that John and Jackson could use. Explain how they could be used to test their idea.** *(6 marks)*

   (c) **John and Jackson are planning to set up as a partnership. Explain THREE benefits of this form of organisation.** *(6 marks)*

   (d) **John's father has advised them to set up a limited company. Explain THREE benefits of this form of organisation.** *(6 marks)*

   (e) **Which form of organisation would you recommend to them? Give reasons for your answer.** *(6 marks)*

Total: 30 marks

Item B

The machine for the car wash costs £15,000. There will also be rent for the site. The friends will also have to buy materials. John and Jackson are going to have to raise the money and are thinking of asking the bank for a loan. The bank has said it will consider this if provided with a business plan.

2 (a) **What is meant by a 'business plan'?** *(2 marks)*

   (b) **Explain THREE ways in which a business plan could be of use to John and Jackson.** *(6 marks)*

   (c) **How could a business plan help John and Jackson to succeed in their business venture? Give reasons to support your views.** *(9 marks)*

Total: 17 marks

Item C

John and Jackson think that they will not be able to staff the business themselves but will need some employees to help them in the business. They want to employ part-time staff to work at the busiest periods, as they think they can cope with demand themselves at other times.

3 (a) **List THREE different ways that John and Jackson could advertise for staff.**

(3 marks)

(b) **Explain the main factors that would make a job advertisement a success.**

(6 marks)

(c) **Explain why good customer service would be vital for the success of the business.**

(4 marks)

Total: 13 marks

Overall total: 60 marks

Unit 2
Growing as a business

Topic 21
Business expansion

What the specification requires

You should understand that there are both benefits and risks of expanding as a business and that sometimes the risks outweigh the benefits. You should know about the different ways in which larger businesses can expand, both internally and externally.

In brief

Businesses can be very small or very large. They range from sole traders with no employees to very large concerns, employing thousands of people. To get from one to the other requires growth. Such expansion brings benefits, but it may also bring drawbacks, so a business has to be certain that it is a good idea for it to get bigger. Many businesses have found very good reasons for staying small, so they do not seek to expand.

Revision notes

- A business can get bigger through either **internal growth** or **external growth**.
- Internal growth is also called organic growth. This is when the business grows larger from within, usually at a gradual pace, by increasing sales, using new technology, widening its product range to expand its markets, or winning a larger share of its main market.

Speak the language

economies of scale — cost benefits from growth

external growth — growth by combining with other business

internal growth — growth from within the business (also called organic growth)

- External growth is when a business grows by joining with other businesses. It can merge with other businesses in an 'agreed marriage'. This is called a merger. Alternatively, it can take over another business in a hostile way. This is called a takeover.
- Businesses can benefit from growth: for example, through **economies of scale**. These include the ability to buy in bulk, or save money on transport. They might also suffer diseconomies of scale, such as breakdowns in communication, or management being seen as far removed from the workers.
- One method of growth is via the franchise route. One business sells the right to use its successful business format to another business, which has to buy the right and pay a percentage of its profits as a royalty.

- Many businesses do not try to grow. They may have just started and be more concerned with survival; they may be reaching their own objectives without getting any bigger; they may be providing a local service; they may be supplying specialist products to small markets.

In a nutshell

* Sometimes a business wants to grow.
* It can achieve growth internally (organically) or externally.
* External growth usually comes through a merger or takeover.
* Takeovers are 'agreed marriages'; they tend to be hostile.
* Growth can bring benefits such as economies of scale.
* It can also bring problems such as breakdowns in communication.
* Not all businesses want to grow.

Boost your grade

AO1: you might have the chance to introduce the idea of *integration* into an answer. This is the technical term for one business joining with another. The types of integration are shown in the diagram. The important thing to remember is what advantages integration might bring — for example, bigger market share, economies of scale, greater specialisation, removing competition and securing supplies.

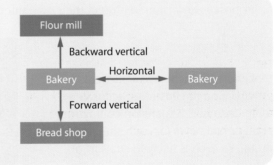

Test yourself

Say whether each statement is true or false.

1 A business can get bigger through either internal growth or external growth.

2 All businesses want to grow.

3 Internal growth is also called organic growth.

4 External growth is also called inorganic growth.

5 Businesses can grow through franchising.

6 Growing businesses do not get economies of scale.

7 Mergers are when two businesses agree to join.

8 Bulk buying is an economy of scale.

9 A royalty is a percentage of profits.

10 Takeovers are when two businesses agree to join.

Topic 22
Stakeholder conflict

What the specification requires

You should understand that expansion can bring benefits and drawbacks. You should know who the stakeholders of a business are and be able to explain how an expansion might affect their interests. You need to consider the ways in which stakeholders might react to expansion or proposed expansion to protect their own interests.

In brief

Stakeholders each have a particular influence on the business, according to their stake in it. Expansion could bring good or bad news for each stakeholder group, so each is likely to support or oppose expansion to protect its own interests. For example, owners such as shareholders could vote against expansion if they think it will reduce the value of shares or their dividends; customers could react by taking custom elsewhere if they feel that their choice has been reduced.

Fotolia

Many groups are affected by the expansion of a business

Revision notes

- Stakeholders have a stake in a business. This stake can be affected by the decision of the business to expand.
- **Internal stakeholders** have a direct interest in the business. They are employed by it or own it, and rely on the business for their income.
- Owners could find their influence diluted by expansion. If expanding means joining with another business, this could mean sharing management. Expansion could mean that shareholders' control is reduced.
- Business expansion may lead to economies of scale. This could mean that fewer employees are needed. Mergers and takeovers often make the new business more efficient, but at a cost to employees.

- **External stakeholders** are people or other businesses that have a less direct stake in a business. For example, the business is located in their community, they buy its products, or they compete with or supply the business.
- An expanded business may offer advantages to some stakeholders, such as bigger orders for suppliers; it may also want better deals (and be able to enforce them).
- Customers may lose out if a competitor is taken over, as they then have reduced choice.
- The community where the business operates may suffer from problems such as more transport and pollution.
- Expansion can cause stakeholder conflicts. For example, customers may want lower prices while shareholders want higher profits; suppliers may want paying immediately while the business wants to delay payment; a business may want to expand operations but the community wants to keep it small. Stakeholders might act to protect their interests.

> **Speak the language**
>
> **internal stakeholders** — those who are directly linked to the business, such as owners and employee
>
> **external stakeholders** — those indirectly linked to the business, such as the community in which the business operates

In a nutshell

* Stakeholders have an interest in a business.
* Expansion can bring each stakeholder problems or benefits.
* Stakeholders will support or resist expansion according to how their power is affected.
* Sometimes this means that stakeholder groups will be in conflict.

Test yourself

Choose the correct answer from the following alternatives.

1 Customers may lose out if a competitor is taken over, as they then have reduced **(a)** choice, **(b)** shops, **(c)** prices, **(d)** control.

2 If the business joins with another business, this could mean which group has to share control? **(a)** owners, **(b)** managers, **(c)** suppliers, **(d)** employees

3 Which group could benefit from expansion through gaining bigger orders? **(a)** owners, **(b)** managers, **(c)** suppliers, **(d)** employees

4 Business expansion may lead to **(a)** economies of scale, **(b)** diseconomies of scale, **(c)** more control for shareholders, **(d)** lower prices.

5 A takeover may mean that fewer of which group are needed? **(a)** owners, **(b)** managers, **(c)** suppliers, **(d)** employees

> **AO1:** AO1 marks are gained for the correct use of knowledge and terms. You should therefore know the difference between internal and external stakeholders and be able to explain this.

Topic 23
Choosing the right legal structure

What the specification requires

You should understand that private limited companies may decide to become public limited companies for a number of reasons. There are benefits and drawbacks to such a move which you should be able to explain. You will not be asked about the legal process of incorporation.

In brief

As this part of the specification is focused on larger businesses, the starting point here is the private limited company. Private limited companies already benefit from limited liability, so the main reason for them to become public is likely to be to raise extra finance. It is also possible, however, for owners to lose control. For some private limited companies, this change in organisation will be an appropriate route to take; for others, drawbacks will outweigh gains.

Setting up a company (note: there are plans by government to make this process even easier.)

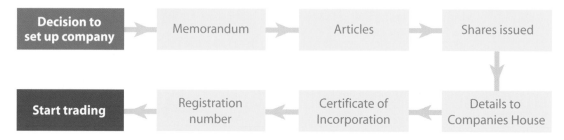

Revision notes

- **Private limited companies** that want to raise large amounts of capital may do so by becoming public limited companies.
- Private limited companies are usually shortened to 'ltd'; **public limited companies** are usually shortened to 'plc'.
- Becoming a plc is neither expensive nor complicated; it involves producing evidence that the business is in good health and reliable.
- Becoming a plc allows the business to offer shares for sale on the stock exchange. It is a good way to raise large amounts of finance. However, a stock exchange listing means

anyone can buy shares — including people or organisations that may put their own interests above those of the business. Competitors that buy shares have information about the business, but also have a say in how it is organised or operated. Public shareholders are often more interested in gaining a quick profit than in the long-term health of the business, so they may buy and sell shares regardless of the strength of the business. This can be a drawback for the plc.

- Plcs also have to publish annual accounts and make them accessible to anyone who requests them. This means that all their strengths and weaknesses can be seen, even by competitors.
- **Shareholders** each have a vote (one per share), so they can affect the decision-making process of the business.

In a nutshell

* Private limited companies may need extra finance to grow.
* One way to raise this is by going public.
* There are advantages to this, such as raising finance.
* There are also disadvantages, such as the possibility of losing control.

Test yourself

Try this exam-style question.

Gerrards plc is a multinational business with branches in over 20 countries. It manufactures and sells drugs. It is quoted on the London Stock Exchange.

1 Give reasons why a business might not wish to 'go public'. *(6 marks)*

2 Give reasons why a person may wish to buy shares in a company. *(4 marks)*

Boost your grade

AO1 to AO2: for AO2 marks you must show that you understand concepts in context. You should only suggest becoming a plc as a way to raise money for a large business that is already succeeding. It is not suitable for start-ups or small businesses.

Changing business aims and objectives

What the specification requires

You need to understand that as a business grows, its aims and objectives are going to change. While a small business may be happy to survive, break even and maybe make a small profit, a larger business might have bigger ambitions.

In brief

Once a business is established and successful, it may look for new opportunities to increase profits. It may also wish to become stronger to protect itself from the possible effects of competition. It may want to grow to become the dominant business in its market. Some businesses decide that they would rather expand overseas, into bigger markets than are available at home in the UK.

Revision notes

- All businesses have **aims** and **objectives** that they are trying to reach. These are likely to be different depending on the size of the business, the market that it is in and the point it has reached in terms of growth. Objectives are often seen as stepping stones on the way to the final aim.
- The initial aims for a small business are survival, **breakeven** and independence. Growing businesses may have achieved these aims and want to increase profits or market share, or produce a greater range of products.
- Growing businesses are likely to have other aims, such as market leadership. This means becoming the dominant business in its market. This is a position that allows it to make more profit and to have control over, for example, suppliers.
- Such dominance can be bad for other businesses competing in the same market and, in the long run, bad for consumers.

Fotolia

Businesses can take advantage of lower labour costs overseas in order to increase profits

- A business may want to expand overseas. If it does, it may face problems of language and communication, currency and different laws. However, the business will try to overcome these because of the advantages that are brought by international expansion. These can include lower production costs through cheaper labour and power costs, lower transport costs and different laws. Such expansion also gives the business access to much wider markets.

Speak the language

aims — long-term targets of the business

breakeven — where total cost equals total revenue

objectives — short-term 'stepping stones' on the way to aims

In a nutshell

* As businesses grow, their aims and objectives will change.
* Key objectives may include market control or an expanded product range.
* Overseas expansion may also be an option.
* This brings some problems and some benefits.

Test yourself

Say whether each statement is true or false.

1 Initial aims for small businesses include survival.

2 All businesses want to grow.

3 Growing businesses may just want to survive.

4 Market leadership is a possible aim for an expanding business.

5 Problems of expansion overseas include communication.

6 Overseas expansion leads to a narrowing of markets.

7 Overseas production can mean lower labour costs.

8 Objectives are the long-term targets of a business.

9 Breakeven is an aim; it is where fixed costs equal revenue.

10 Different laws in foreign countries can cause problems for businesses.

Boost your grade

AO2 to AO3: once you have given an explanation or analysed a situation, you may be asked to make a judgement. For example, should a business that has grown stick with its current suppliers out of loyalty, or move to cheaper ones? It doesn't matter about your conclusion — to boost your grade from AO2 to AO3, the important thing is to support it with reasons.

Ethics and the environment

What the specification requires

You should understand that some of the costs and benefits of business are social costs and benefits. These are those that are carried by society as a whole. It is in the interests of businesses to have ethical policies and to reduce environmental problems. Such areas are often built into a company's aims and objectives.

In brief

Businesses can bring both benefits and disadvantages to the communities within which they operate. Some businesses may be noisy, or require heavy transport; some may deal in dangerous products or produce unpleasant waste products. Many businesses are able to regulate themselves, to make sure that the bad effects of their business do not upset the local community, and include environmental targets in their objectives. The government has also passed laws to make sure that businesses do not damage the environment or present a danger to communities.

Revision notes

- There are so many advantages to businesses of being environmentally responsible that many do much more than government legislation makes them. The advantages include greater efficiency and lower costs, as well as the increased custom that comes from a better reputation. Being seen as **environmentally friendly** may be one of the main objectives of a business.
- Businesses should also act in ethical ways — that is, they should be moral in their actions.
- The main **social costs** created by businesses are pollution (air, water, noise, visual, etc.), safety hazards — from increased traffic, or because of the nature of the business itself — and waste products. Apart from waste discharged into the air or water, many businesses produce other waste products that are either dangerous or difficult to cope with.

> **Speak the language**
>
> **carbon footprint** — the amount of carbon (and therefore environmental damage) released through an activity
>
> **environmentally friendly** — not harming the environment
>
> **social costs** — costs that affect the whole community, such as pollution

Pollution is a major social cost created by businesses

- Many businesses have recognised the effect that their business can have on the local, national and international environment, and have taken steps to reduce the impact. Many businesses also take advantage of these steps in their marketing. They let customers know of their environmental concern in the hopes that this will increase sales.
- The most common methods of reducing **carbon footprint** are:
  - recycling paper and packaging, and using recycled paper for packaging
  - only using timber from sustainable forests — those managed in an environmental way
  - fitting pollutant controls (such as smoke filters) wherever possible
  - using 'green' fuels in vehicles that have high performance in terms of miles per litre, and are fitted with pollution reduction devices such as catalytic converters
  - energy-saving policies such as lighting systems that switch on and off only when areas are in use

In a nutshell

* Businesses can bring problems as well as benefits to communities.
* Many of these involve environmental costs, such as pollution.
* Environmentally friendly businesses aim to minimise these problems.
* Ethical businesses act in a moral way, 'doing the right thing'.
* As this enhances reputation and may lower costs, it is also good for business.

Test yourself

Fill in the missing words using the list below to describe environmentally responsible business. If you are feeling confident, cover the words and do the exercise from memory.

Businesses can bring both benefits and .... to the .... within which they operate. Although businesses may provide jobs, they may also cause ...., such as ....

Many businesses regulate themselves, to make sure that the bad effects of their business do not upset the .... Often they include environmental targets in their .... The advantages of being .... include greater .... and lower .... There is also the increased custom due to having a better ....

communities   costs   disadvantages   efficiency   environmentally friendly

local community   objectives   pollution   reputation   social costs

Topic 26
Location and larger businesses

What the specification requires

You should know that, if a business is growing, it may have to change its location. For any location that it chooses, the aim should be to keep costs down and increase revenues. Businesses that decide to locate overseas will have a further set of decisions to take, which could affect costs and revenues.

In brief

As a business grows, it may feel that its location is no longer suitable. In particular, it may find that it needs more space for operations, storage and transport. Should it decide to trade overseas, it may have to face all the costs and difficulties of setting up in a foreign country. The major decision will be whether to export from the UK, or to move production abroad. Costs abroad could be lower, but there could also be disadvantages, such as operating under different laws.

Revision notes

Growing businesses may need more space for storage

- Growing businesses may need to rethink their location. They may need more space, better access to transport, or more power. For example, if production levels increase, they may need more indoor space for production and storage, and more outside space for transport and deliveries. They may need better links to **infrastructure** such as water, power, transport, communications and other services. An expanding business has to answer questions about the space it needs, the infrastructure links, facilities such as IT and the availability of skilled labour.
- Businesses that relocate will usually do so with the aim of reducing their costs and increasing their revenues.
- Businesses which rely heavily on raw materials will still have to be near their source. Businesses that provide a service are likely to be nearer their market.

Fotolia

- Should a business expand globally, there are other considerations regarding its location. A major decision to take is whether to use **agents** in foreign countries, or whether to set up its own offices.
- If a business expands to an overseas location, it must comply with local laws and regulations, and be prepared to conduct business in the language of the host country.
- If it decides to export products, it may need to be nearer a transport hub, or to a port or airport.
- For some businesses, location is unimportant. This is true of many web-based businesses — although they will still need access to a distribution system, even if that is only the postal system.

In a nutshell

* Growing businesses may need new, larger locations.
* They may also need more locations.
* Some of these may be overseas.
* Factors such as transport links, availability of power and other infrastructure are important.
* Some businesses may need to be close to raw materials; others to customers.

Test yourself

Try this exam-style question.

Samson plc is based in Bristol. It sells running shoes and trainers. It has just received a large order from the USA. It could either make the shoes in Bristol and export them to the USA or set up a plant in the USA.

Which would you recommend?
Give reasons for your answer.   *(9 marks)*

AO2 to AO3: once you have given an explanation or analysed a situation (AO2), you may be asked to make a judgement (AO3). For example, should this expanding business increase home production and export or set up production overseas? It doesn't matter what your conclusion is — the important thing is to support it with reasons.

Section test: Business organisation

Read Item A and then answer the questions that follow.

Item A

Curacell Ltd is a supermarket chain in the UK. It has a large share of the market but plans to expand further. It has set itself a number of objectives to help with this. The expansion will need to be financed, so, at a recent meeting, the directors discussed whether to 'float' the company on the stock exchange.

1 What is an 'objective'?   *(1 mark)*

2 Suggest TWO possible objectives for Curacell Ltd.   *(4 marks)*

3 Should the business 'float' on the stock exchange as some of the directors suggested, or remain a private limited company? Recommend a course of action to Curacell. Give reasons for your answer.   *(9 marks)*

Read Item B and then answer the questions that follow.

Item B

Curacell has a reputation as an environmentally friendly concern. It uses recycled cardboard for all its packaging. This is also cheaper than new cardboard. It has a 'green' transport fleet that runs on low emission fuel. It also makes sure that its lorries are always fully loaded. This helps to keep down costs.

4 Explain THREE ways in which the supermarket has gained from its environmental policies.   *(6 marks)*

Total: 20 marks

Topic 27
Advanced marketing mix: product

What the specification requires

You should understand that, as a business grows, it may wish to expand its product portfolio. You should know that, as the demand for a good or service changes over time, there is a natural 'life cycle' and the business may try to extend this life cycle.

In brief

As a business grows, it can compete more effectively by offering a wider range of products. As demand for a product changes, it passes through a life cycle, starting with the launch of the product and ending with its withdrawal from the market. Businesses can use various ways to try to extend the product life cycle, if they think the product will still sell. These methods will have an impact on the costs and revenues of the business, and its ability to compete with its other products.

Revision notes

- The **product portfolio** refers to the various products a business offers for sale. As a business grows, it can increase its portfolio to create a wider range. A wider and more balanced range helps it to compete.
- The **product life cycle** shows the usual stages through which a product passes. Like a person, a product is born, grows old, matures and eventually dies. Some life cycles are very short, or explosive. Others are very long or extended. The stage of the life cycle is important to a business. It shows it what sort of promotion or other changes might be needed to boost sales.

Sainsbury's

Sainsbury's 'Taste the difference' product range

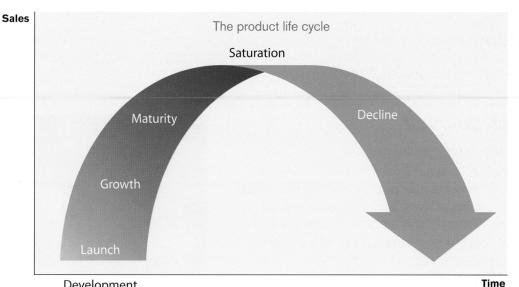

Sales

The product life cycle

Saturation

Maturity

Decline

Growth

Launch

Development

Time

- The normal product life cycle is shown above. Each stage can be for a short or a long time. This will differ from product to product. The stages in the life cycle are:
  - development — during which no sales are made, but there are costs
  - launch — when the product is first offered for sale; costs can be high as the product needs to be advertised
  - growth — as sales grow, competitors will begin to think about bringing out rival products
  - maturity — many people have bought the product but there are also now competitors; promotion is still needed
  - decline — sales fall and the business must decide whether to try to extend the life cycle or let the product die
- Successful products can have their life cycle extended through product **extension strategies**. These may be changes to the product; finding new uses or applications; or additional promotion. They could add costs to the business but should also increase sales.

> ### Speak the language
>
> **extension strategy** — a way to make the life cycle longer
>
> **product life cycle** — the way in which a product is born, grows and dies
>
> **product portfolio** — the range of products offered by a business

In a nutshell

* Growing businesses can broaden their product portfolio.
* This helps them to compete.
* All products pass through a life cycle.
* Businesses use different ways to support the product at different stages.
* Product extension strategies can be used to extend the life of the product.

Test yourself

Try this exam-style question.

Cosy Candles is a company that sells a range of natural products. One product was very successful for a number of years, but recently demand has fallen off sharply as it appears that either tastes have changed, or everyone has bought enough of this product.

Fotolia

1 Suggest two possible courses of action that Cosy Candles could take with regard to this product. *(6 marks)*

2 What course would you recommend? Give reasons for your answer. *(3 marks)*

Topic 28
Advanced marketing mix: price

What the specification requires

Price is just one part of the marketing mix, but it can be used to support business growth. Various pricing strategies can be used by a growing business to gain market share, or to compete more effectively. You should understand the factors that influence such pricing decisions.

In brief

Larger businesses can use more effective **pricing techniques** than smaller businesses in order to increase market share and further their growth. Different pricing decisions may be used, and how effective they are depends on the type of market and degree of competition in which the business operates. Businesses still have to set prices so that they are competing, and cover their costs. Larger businesses are able to take a loss on certain products for a period, and this makes them more effective competitors in a market.

Fotolia

A £5,000 wedding dress: how much is cost, how much is mark-up?

Revision notes

- The most common form of pricing is **cost-plus pricing**. This is where the business adds up the various costs of producing the product and then adds on a percentage for profit (called a **mark-up**).

Topic 29
Advanced marketing mix: promotion

What the specification requires

You should know that promotional activities can be used to help and support growth. Growing businesses can choose from a greater range of appropriate promotional methods than small businesses. Businesses need to choose promotions carefully, taking into account the product itself, the market in which they are operating and the likely reaction of competitors.

In brief

Larger businesses may have more effective promotional strategies, firstly because they can afford them, and secondly because, as they grow larger, they need to use them to reach wider markets. Methods that are not suitable for smaller businesses, such as television or national billboard campaigns, are more expensive but may also be more effective. Any method used will be effective only if it is appropriate to the product and effective in the market. The use of promotion in a competitive market may be countered by other businesses increasing their own levels of promotion.

Revision notes

- Growing businesses are able to afford a much greater range of **promotional strategies** than small businesses. Advertising is publicity for a product that is paid for directly; it is called **above-the-line** expenditure. Advertising is used to promote products through broadcast and print media such as television, radio, posters, magazines, leaflets and point-of-sale material. Larger businesses can afford to use outlets such as television. Such outlets tend to be more effective as they reach a wider audience. However, they are also more expensive.

Speak the language

above-the-line — directly paid-for advertising

below-the-line — promotions that increase sales, but are not advertising

promotional strategies — methods designed to increase awareness and sales of a product

Topfoto

Formula One racing is heavily sponsored

- Sales promotion is called **below-the-line** expenditure. Growing businesses can use sales promotion techniques such as loss leaders (see Topic 28), special offers (such as buy one, get one free), competitions, money-off coupons, free samples and trials, joint promotions with other businesses (for example, washing powders recommended by washing machine manufacturers) and loyalty cards. Growing businesses may also be able to market and sell directly to the customer, through websites or catalogues, for example. This is called direct marketing.
- Sponsorship means that the product will be associated with a certain event or sport or what is good about the event — a marathon race could promote fitness, for instance. Larger businesses can afford to sponsor larger and more recognised teams, events or organisations.
- The business should choose the promotional mix that is going to be most effective in its target market. This depends on the nature of the market (for example, is it a market leader? does it have power in the market?), the type of product (for example, is it essential or easily substituted?), and how competitors react to increased promotion.

- *Telesales*. These are where products are sold directly to consumers via a telephone call. Often these are to sell additional products to those already owned, such as additional insurance or a new banking service. **Cold calls** do not tend to be very effective.
- *Mail order*. This is where a business provides a catalogue or advertises in a newspaper or magazine. Such direct sales are only possible where delivery costs are not a major factor.

Internet sales have opened up markets worldwide

- With internet sales, products are delivered to buyers. The product range can be viewed via a website. Websites open up worldwide markets but, again, delivery costs may be a major factor.
- To judge whether or not a distribution channel is appropriate, a business must consider the needs of itself and its customers. Important factors for the business are cost, availability and profit margins. Important factors for customers are convenience, cost and reliability.

In a nutshell

* Growing businesses may need to access more customers.
* To do this, they may need more distribution channels.
* This could mean more traditional channels, such as retailers.
* It may mean more modern channels, such as the internet.

Test yourself

Try this exam-style question,

Cosy Candles is a company that sells a range of natural products. It has a website which tells visitors the location of the nearest outlet and provides details of the range of goods on offer. Customers can buy a limited range of goods from the site. Cosy Candles thinks it should increase the range of goods available.

Analyse the advantages and disadvantages for Cosy Candles of increasing the range of goods it sells on its website.
(6 marks)

Section test: Marketing

Read Item A and then answer the questions that follow.

Item A

Cats & Co. sells a range of mugs, T-towels, placemats and linen, all printed up with distinctive cat logos and designs. It sells these through garden centres, supermarkets and other retail outlets. Recently it has started to face competition from an American manufacturer of similar products called KittyKo. Cats & Co. is worried that its product portfolio may be too narrow to compete.

1 What is a 'product portfolio'? *(1 mark)*

2 Explain THREE ways for Cats & Co. to extend its product portfolio. *(6 marks)*

3 Explain TWO ways in which Cats & Co. could compete more effectively than smaller competitors. *(4 marks)*

4 Suggest TWO possible pricing methods that Cats & Co. could use to compete. Which would you recommend? Give reasons for your answer. *(9 marks)*

Total: 20 marks

Financial statements: profit and loss account

What the specification requires

The profit and loss account lets all stakeholders know how well a business is doing. It shows the operational side of the business. You should be able to identify the various parts of the account, and you should be able to make judgements about the performance of a business, using the account. You will be given relevant formulae whenever they are needed.

In brief

The profit and loss account shows the trading activities of a business. Although referred to as the profit and loss account, there are three parts to it. One part shows trading, one shows the

Sales revenue is recorded in the trading account, one of the three parts of the profit and loss account

profit or loss result of that trading, and one shows where any profit has been distributed. You will need to be able to use the accounts to judge the success of a business and recommend possible courses of action to improve its performance.

Note that under International Financial Reporting Standards, there are different terms for some parts of the account. These are shown in brackets. Both sets of terms will be used for the first few years of the examination.

Revision notes

- There are three parts to the profit and loss account.
- The **trading account** shows what the business has sold and what it has cost for these sales. It shows the income the business has earned. The biggest source for most businesses is sales revenue. From this total, however, the cost of buying or making the product has to be deducted. This is called 'cost of sales'. If you buy 10 pencils at 8p each and sell them at 10p each, your revenue is 10 × 10p = £1, cost of sales is 10 × 8p = 80p, and your gross profit is 20p.
The only time this is different is if you have stocks (inventories) left over. This is your 'opening stock' for the next period. If you only sell 9 pencils, your revenue is 90p, cost of sales is still 80p and gross profit 10p, but you have 1 pencil still in stock.
- The **profit and loss account** shows operating profit. Buying and selling stock costs money. This is called 'expenses'. A business will also have to pay items such as wages, rent on premises, power bills and equipment costs. Gross profit is the amount that you have made before expenses are taken into account. What remains is net (operating) profit.
- The **appropriation account** shows where the net profit has gone. Some of it goes in taxes, some may be given to shareholders in the form of dividends, and some may be kept to help the finances of the business.
- Stakeholders use the profit and loss account to compare profitability with previous periods and other businesses. It also helps managers to plan.

TRADING ACCOUNT		£000	£000
Sales revenue			5,000
minus Cost of sales	Opening inventories	1,000	
	plus Purchases	2,000	
	less Closing inventories	500	2,500
Gross profit			2,500

PROFIT AND LOSS ACCOUNT			
Gross profit			2,500
minus Expenses	Rent	250	
	Wages	250	
	Transport	200	
	Power	100	
	Equipment	200	1,000
Net profit			1,500

APPROPRIATION ACCOUNT		
Net profit		1,500
minus Taxation		500
Profit after taxation		1,000
minus Dividends paid		500
Retained profit		500

Sample profit and loss account

- It is called the balance sheet because both sides must be equal. This is because they are measuring the same things. Think about what you own and owe. These are your assets and liabilities. The amount borrowed or earned to buy these assets must equal what you paid for them. It is the same with a business. There are three parts to a balance sheet. Each is linked to the others. They are:

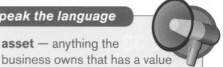
  – *Assets* — all the things that the business owns as either fixed assets (non-current assets), such as buildings and machinery used in production, or current assets, such as stocks (inventories) of finished product that could be easily turned into cash.
  – *Liabilities* — all the things that a business owes, such as current debts that must be paid back within a year, like bank overdrafts or creditors, or long-term liabilities (non-current liabilities) with more than a year before they must be repaid, such as long-term loans and mortgages. Take the liabilities away from the assets and what is left is what the business is worth at this moment. This is called *net current assets*.
  – *Capital* — a final part of the account showing how the money for these net current assets was raised. This could be via shareholders' funds (total equity), profit, or profit made in previous periods (reserves).

In a nutshell

* The balance sheet shows the wealth of a business.
* It shows its ability to pay its debts at a point in time.
* This is the balance of what it owns as against what it owes.
* It is taken at a certain point in time, so is often called a 'snapshot'.
* It is used as a comparison with previous snapshots and other businesses.

Test yourself

State whether each of the following is an asset or a liability.

1 Cash in hand	6 Furniture
2 Cash in the bank	7 Machinery
3 Creditors	8 Overdraft
4 Debtors	9 Stock
5 Factory	10 Vehicles

Topic 34
Ratios

What the specification requires

You should be able to make judgements about the performance of a business by interpreting the information contained in simplified versions of the profit and loss accounts and balance sheet, and by extracting figures to calculate ratios. You should be able to make recommendations using the figures that you have calculated. You will be given relevant formulae whenever they are needed.

In brief

Ratios are important tools in business. A business needs to know how much profit it is making in terms of sales and how much this is really worth when expenses are taken off. It needs to know its true position in terms of its ability to pay debts that are about to become due, by using the acid test ratio to see if it could meet its obligations even if stock went unsold. You should remember what constitutes a healthy range for a ratio and be able to comment on figures accordingly.

Revision notes

- A **ratio** is one thing measured in terms of another, often expressed as a percentage, as it is easier to compare percentage figures.
- **Profitability ratios** measure how much profit the business is making compared to revenue. A business making £10,000 gross profit on £15,000 of sales has a gross profit margin of: 10,000/15,000 × 100 = 66.66%, i.e. £66.66 gross profit for every £100 of sales. The net profit to sales ratio or operating profit margin takes expenses into account. Assuming this business had expenses of £8,000, the operating margin would then be: 2,000/15,000 × 100 = 13.3%.

Fotolia

What is the ratio of boys to girls in your class?

- **Liquidity ratios** look at how easily a business can pay its short-term debts from its assets. These figures are taken from the balance sheet. Current assets divided by current liabilities give the current ratio. A business with current assets of £20,000 and current liabilities of £5,000 would have a current ratio of 20,000/5,000:1 = 4:1 It can cover its debts four times over. A current ratio of between 1.5:1 and 3:1 is considered healthy. A ratio of 4:1 means the business is not making efficient use of its assets.

- For many businesses, some current assets will be stock (inventories) waiting to be sold. This might not happen, so stock has to be taken out of the equation. If the business in the example had £16,000 worth of stock, then (20,000 – 16,000)/5000:1 reduces to 4/5:1 or 0.8:1. This means the business has just 80p with which to pay every £1 of short-term debt, unless it sells some stock. This is called the acid test ratio and measures the real ability of a business to pay its debts. An acid test ratio of between 1.5:1 and 3:1 is considered healthy. This business is carrying too much of its assets in stock.

In a nutshell

* Ratios are useful for seeing how well something is performing.
* They can be applied to liquidity and profitability.
* They can be used to compare performance over time.
* They can be used to make comparisons with similar businesses.

Test yourself

Try this exam-style question.

Alberus plc is a well-known chain of high-street shops, selling a range of goods, including clothes, food and household goods. This is an extract from its accounts (figures in £m).

Year	2010	2009	2008
Fixed assets	2,500	2,400	2,350
Current assets	2,700	2,600	2,450
Current liabilities	900	850	750
Net current assets	1,800	1,750	1,700

1 Calculate the current ratio for 2010. Show your working. *(3 marks)*

2 Should Alberus be concerned about this figure? *(3 marks)*

3 Explain a possible difficulty that the business might face if it had a very low current ratio. *(4 marks)*

Boost your grade

AO1/2 to AO3: while it is easy to work ratios out, it is more important to make sure that they are properly interpreted. From year to year, they can be used to compare how well the business is doing. In any one year, they can show whether the business is in a strong or weak position.

Section test: Finance

Read Item A and then answer the questions that follow.

Item A

KittyKo wants to know if it is performing better in 2010 than it did in 2009. It has the following figures available (all in £m).

	2010	2009
Revenue	115	100
Gross profit	80	60
Net profit	8	9

1 Calculate gross profit margin for 2009 and 2010. *(3 marks)*

2 Calculate net profit margin (operating margin) for 2009 and 2010. *(3 marks)*

3 Using your figures, and your own knowledge, say whether KittyKo is doing better in 2010 than 2009. *(5 marks)*

4 Suggest TWO ways in which KittyKo could improve performance. Recommend one of these ways to the business, giving reasons to support your judgement. *(9 marks)*

Total: 20 marks

Boost your grade

AO1 to AO2: organisational structures often have in-built inefficiencies because of the way a business has developed: for instance, growth has left managers in charge of departments that are too large. Use this reasoning in the context of the case study business to support your knowledge and achieve AO2 marks.

Test yourself

Match the statement on the right with the correct term on the left.

1 authority — diagram showing relationships in a business

2 centralisation — the number of people for whom a manager is responsible

3 decentralisation — the right to pass on authority to others

4 delegation — decisions made by a few people

5 manager — decisions spread throughout the organisation

6 organisational chart — those over whom someone else has power

7 span of contron — decision-making power

8 subordinates — a person with authority

Topic 36
Recruitment and retention of staff

What the specification requires

You should understand that, as businesses grow, they need to recruit more staff. Such recruitment and selection must be fair and legal. Once recruited, staff may need to be trained for both their own benefit and for that of the business. Induction training is vital for all new staff, and further training increases the value of employees by making them more effective.

In brief

In recruitment, businesses must conform to the law. Advertising (and the whole process of recruiting) must be fair and open; all groups must be treated equally. Businesses will need to follow a set recruitment procedure to make sure that they are being fair to everyone. Discrimination in the recruitment process is illegal. Training can be done at the place of work, or be conducted by external bodies off-site. There are advantages and disadvantages to both methods.

Revision notes

- Set procedures ensure that the process of advertising and selection, usually by interview, is legal and fair.
- Once appointed, new staff need an **induction training** programme. This is training to introduce staff to the workplace and the job. It will include basic training in processes and methods, and will also let the new employee know the **custom and practice** in the business, such as when breaks or holiday can be taken. It will introduce staff to machinery and its operation, outline responsibilities and inform them about their **line manager**. It will also let them know the rules and regulations (such as health and safety) and what to do in case of a problem or dispute.

Fotolia

Large businesses often have their own training departments

- Further training will improve staff efficiency. It is therefore of benefit to the business. It is also development for the employee, making him or her more valuable.
- Businesses have to decide whether to carry out training themselves, or use external agencies. Big businesses are likely to have their own training departments that have an in-depth knowledge of the needs of the business. Big businesses may also choose to use agencies, as will smaller businesses.
- Agencies can be more effective at training, but tend to be expensive. Some of the most effective training may be on-the-job training. This is where the employee is taught as he or she carries out the job. This makes for good training but may reduce effectiveness while it is taking place. Alternatively, off-the-job training could take place using an external trainer, off-site.

Speak the language

custom and practice — what is accepted as normal in a business

induction training — training to introduce a worker to a business

line manager — the manager immediately in charge of an employee

In a nutshell

* Growing businesses need to appoint staff.
* New recruits need induction training.
* Further training will enhance the value of staff.
* This could be carried out by the business or an agency.
* It could be on-the-job or off-the-job training.
* Appraisal allows both employer and manager to review progress.
* This is just one of a number of ways to motivate staff.

Test yourself

Choose the correct answers from the following alternatives.

1 The process to develop the skills and knowledge that the business needs is called **(a)** training, **(b)** advertising, **(c)** interviewing, **(d)** development.

2 The process to develop the skills and knowledge that the employee needs is called **(a)** recruitment, **(b)** training, **(c)** interviewing, **(d)** development.

3 The initial introduction to a business is usually called **(a)** initial training, **(b)** introduction training, **(c)** induction training, **(d)** initial development.

4 The process of training provides which of the following for a worker? **(a)** praise, **(b)** induction, **(c)** personal development, **(d)** appraisal

5 Training that takes place at the place of work is called **(a)** at the job, **(b)** with the job, **(c)** on the job, **(d)** off the job.

Boost your grade

AO1 to AO2: you should be able not just to describe what is meant by induction training but, in the context of a given business, suggest an appropriate training programme. Make sure that you give examples from the case study business: for example, customer service training for a retail business; health and hygiene training for a food business.

Topic 37
Appraisal and performance review

What the specification requires

You should understand how appraisal can be used to support training and staff development. You should realise that an appraisal and performance management can be a way of motivating staff. You should understand that motivation may also come from financial schemes such as bonuses or profit sharing.

In brief

Training and appraisal are ways to show staff that they are valued, so they can help with motivation. Appraisal is a way for both employer and employee to share views, to consider what has happened in the past and, just as importantly, to plan targets for the future. The use of different styles of management in different situations can also help motivate employees to be more effective in their roles.

Revision notes

- **Appraisal** is a process used to see how well a worker is doing. It also allows the worker to exchange views with the employer. A good appraisal may result in rewards, or may be part of the path to promotion, so it can be used to motivate. Performance management reviews are not as two-way as appraisals, tending to focus on the employer's view.

Appraisals are a two-way process

- Appraisal and performance management systems are often built in to the organisation of businesses, as they are recognised as a way to increase efficiency.
- Businesses that have invested a lot of time in training and development will want to retain staff and may operate a system of financial or other rewards (such as recognition and increased responsibility) in order to do so. Appraisal can help to identify where progress has been made. Retention is cheaper and more effective than making new appointments.
- There may also be financial rewards designed to motivate. Examples include performance-related bonuses and **profit-sharing** schemes. Non-financial rewards such as praise and recognition can also be effective.

- Managers can use a number of different styles of management. The most common of these are:
  - *Autocratic* — managers make decisions on their own and tell others what to do. This has the advantage of showing clear leadership but may upset people.
  - *Democratic* — managers involve others in decision making. This helps people to feel involved but could lead to poor decisions.
  - *Laissez-faire* — managers allow **subordinates** to make their own decisions. This can be seen as giving workers power but can produce poor decisions.
  - *Bureaucratic* — managers follow the rulebook. This is inflexible, but everyone knows where they stand.
- Better managers choose the style to suit the situation: for example, a more direct style for a job that is urgent.

Speak the language

appraisal — a two-way process between employee and manager, to share views and check on progress

profit sharing — where employees receive a bonus based on profit made

subordinate — an employee over whom someone has authority

In a nutshell

* Appraisal allows both employer and manager to review progress.
* This is just one of a number of ways to motivate staff.
* Financial and non-financial rewards can be used to motivate.
* Managers should be flexible in their choice of management style.

Boost your grade

AO1 to AO2: you will not be asked about specific motivational theories, but should you know any, this would show a good depth of knowledge and understanding.

Test yourself

Fill in the missing words using the list below . If you are feeling confident, cover the words and do the exercise from memory.

Two processes used to see how well a worker is doing are called .... and .... The processes may allow the .... to exchange views with the .... A good appraisal may result in ...., or may be part of the path to promotion, so can be used to .... These processes are often built in to the organisation of businesses, as they are recognised as a way to increase .... Businesses that have invested a lot of time in .... and .... will want to .... staff as this is cheaper and more .... than constantly making new appointments.

appraisal   development   effective   efficiency   employees   employer   motivate   performance management review   retain   rewards   training

Section test: People in business

Read Item A and then answer the questions that follow.

Item A

Hepworths is a small chain of butchers shops in Yorkshire. It has just bought premises in Lancashire and is opening two new branches. The new staff will need to be trained by an external agency before they can work with meat products.

1 Explain what sort of training is involved if an external agency is used. *(2 marks)*

2 Suggest whether or not this is the best way to train new staff. *(4 marks)*

3 What is an induction programme? Draw up an induction programme for staff at the new branches. *(4 marks)*

4 Explain two benefits of training to:
   (a) the business
   (b) the employee *(6 marks)*

5 Training is said to motivate staff. Explain whether you agree with this statement, and why. *(4 marks)*

Total: 20 marks

Topic 38
Production methods for growing businesses

What the specification requires

You will need to know that flow production is only available to large businesses and that it gives them the advantage of specialisation and division of labour. You should recognise that efficiency for a business could mean boredom and deskilling for workers. You should know about lean production techniques and their effect on efficiency.

In brief

Only larger businesses can use flow production and therefore benefit from **specialisation**. You should recognise, however, that there are advantages and disadvantages to specialisation and division of labour. Workers can be very good at a specific task, but can become bored and deskilled and lose interest in their work. Production can also be made more efficient through the use of lean production techniques, but staff may struggle with them if they are put under pressure. There are therefore implications for training staff and keeping them motivated.

Revision notes

- Production describes how raw materials and other inputs such as components are turned into outputs — the product. The method of production will depend on the nature of the product and the nature of the customer.

- Larger businesses will be able to use **flow production**. This involves a product being assembled, processed or built as it moves along a production line. Examples are car manufacture (production line) and oil refining (processing). Flow production allows modern businesses to use specialisation and automation. Some processes can even be carried out by robots.

- Flow production allows **division of labour** to be used. Each worker can specialise on a particular task. This makes them more efficient. It may also demotivate them through boredom.

Ingram

Machines can be used efficiently on a production line

- **Lean production** is the idea that a business can be more efficient by minimising the use of all the inputs necessary for production. A business can cut down on all inputs but, perhaps most importantly, on time.
- The main version of lean production is the **just-in-time** (JIT) approach. Parts, components and other materials arrive just as they are needed. There is therefore no need for stock to be held, or for a business to have the costs of storage. Of course, this means an efficient distribution system is essential. If stock or parts do not arrive in time, the whole process is stopped.
- Working to tight deadlines can be difficult and mistakes can be made. Working under pressure could demotivate staff. Workers need proper training to cope with such systems.

Speak the language

division of labour — dividing work (and workers) up to specialise on a particular task

flow production — a product being assembled, processed or built as it moves along a production line

just-in-time — a version of lean production where materials arrive just as they are needed

lean production — minimising the use of all the inputs necessary for production

specialisation — when a worker concentrates on a particular task

In a nutshell

* Larger businesses can use flow production.
* This lets them benefit from specialisation and division of labour.
* This can also have drawbacks for workers.
* Large businesses can also use lean production techniques.
* There are implications for staff motivation and training when such systems are used.

Test yourself

Choose the correct answers from the following alternatives.

1 The production method when parts etc. arrive only as they are needed is called **(a)** test-in-time, **(b)** just-in-time, **(c)** batch production, **(d)** mean production.

2 Production that cuts down on the use of workers, but can use more machinery is called **(a)** job production, **(b)** flow production, **(c)** batch production, **(d)** lean production.

3 Producing large quantities of a product on a production line is called **(a)** job production, **(b)** flow production, **(c)** batch production, **(d)** lean production.

4 Division of labour allows which of the following to be used? **(a)** specialisation, **(b)** delegation, **(c)** job production, **(d)** induction.

5 Efficient production, using the minimum number of inputs, is called **(a)** job production, **(b)** flow production, **(c)** batch production, **(d)** lean production.

AO1 to AO2: the main difference between production in this unit and what you have already learned in Unit 1 is that bigger businesses can use flow production and other lean production techniques. To achieve AO2 marks, therefore, you must make sure that your answers use the business that you are given in the case study

Recognising the challenges of growth

What the specification requires

As a business gets bigger, it is able to benefit from cost advantages over its smaller competitors. Many of these advantages are called **economies of scale**. There are also disadvantages to growth, such as longer chains of communication, more remote management and more complex production processes.

In brief

Businesses that grow to a certain size can begin to benefit from economies of scale, such as buying in **bulk**, using bigger and better machinery and using specialist managers. Many of these are within the control of the business, so are internal. There may also be disadvantages or diseconomies of scale, most of which are linked to communication or organisation. More complicated production processes may also bring problems. Businesses can also gain from the growth of their own industry.

Revision notes

- When a business grows, it has the chance to gain the benefits of economies of scale. These are benefits that a business can gain by, for example, buying in bulk, or producing in larger numbers. Diseconomies are when the growth of the business causes problems.
- There may be internal economies of scale within the business. The main economies are:
  - *Financial* — cost savings through lenders treating them as lower risk.
  - *Bulk buying* — obtaining lower prices by buying inputs in large amounts.
  - *Technical* — the use of specialist machines and workers.

Fotolia

Buying paper in bulk, for example, keeps prices low

- Bigger businesses can also spread risk over a larger output and over a greater variety of output, diversifying into other products and markets.
- There can be disadvantages to growth. Managers may become less efficient and more remote from the business's operations, making them less effective. The management structure is likely to become more complex and therefore unwieldy. Lines of communication can become stretched and decision making less efficient. Workers may feel remote from the hub of the organisation. This can mean that they are less loyal than they are likely to be in a smaller business.
- Specialisation may lead to industrial disputes if workers are bored or undervalued.
- External economies may arise from the growth of an industry. The business may be able to attract skilled labour and managers, and specialised ancillary businesses providing components, raw materials and services to the industry.

Speak the language

bulk — a large amount

economies of scale — benefits gained from the growth of a business

In a nutshell

* Businesses that grow big enough can benefit from economies of scale.
* Most of these economies are internal.
* There may also be diseconomies linked to growth.
* These include poor communication and more remote management.
* Businesses can also gain externally, from the growth of their industry.

Boost your grade

AO1 to AO2: economies of scale are, by definition, only available to big businesses, so you must make sure that the business you have been given is big enough to benefit from them.

Test yourself

Match the economies of scale on the left with the correct description on the right.

1 bulk buying — arising from the growth of a business
2 external — cost savings through lenders treating them as lower risk
3 financial — arising from the growth of an industry
4 internal — using specialist machines and workers
5 technical — lower prices by buying inputs in large amounts

- The **profit and loss account** shows operating profit. Buying and selling stock costs money. This is called expenses. A business will also have to pay items such as wages, rent on premises, power bills and equipment costs. Gross profit is the amount that you have made before expenses are taken into account. What remains is net (operating) profit.
- The **appropriation account** shows where the net profit has gone. Some of it goes in taxes, some may be given to shareholders in the form of dividends, and some may be kept to help the finances of the business.
- Stakeholders use the profit and loss account to compare profitability with previous periods and other businesses. It also helps managers to plan.

Speak the language

appropriation account — shows where the net profit (operating profit) has gone

profit and loss account — the operational record of the business

trading account — what the business has sold and what it has cost for these sales

In a nutshell

* The profit and loss account shows the operational side of the business.
* It shows its trading position.
* It shows how much profit or loss has been made from that trading.
* It shows where profit has been distributed.

Boost your grade **AO1 to AO2:** you will be asked to calculate some of the figures from financial accounts. There are three things to remember: always use a calculator; estimate your answers first to make sure you are not several zeros out; show your workings.

Test yourself

Delete the plus/minus alternatives that do not apply, then complete the account.

Trading account	£000		£000
Sales revenue			20,000
plus/minus Cost of sales	Opening inventories	12,000	
	plus/minus		
	Purchases	5,500	
	plus/minus		
	Closing inventories	2,000 =	?
Gross profit			?
plus/minus Expenses	Rent	500	
	Wages	2,000	
	Transport	750	
	Power	500	
	Equipment	500 =	?
Net profit/loss			?

The amount of profit/loss is therefore £ _____

What the specification requires

You should know that the balance sheet shows the financial position of a business, in terms of its wealth, at a particular point in time. It shows what the business owns as against what it owes. You will need to identify the various parts of the account and how they are calculated. You should recognise the importance of the balance sheet to stakeholders. You will be given relevant formulae whenever they are needed.

In brief

The balance sheet shows the wealth of a business. It measures **assets** against **liabilities**. It will always balance, as the liabilities have been used to purchase the assets. Balance sheets can be used to show levels of debt and financial security for the business.

Note that under International Financial Reporting Standards, there are different terms for some parts of the account. These are shown in brackets. Both will be used for the first few years of the examination.

Revision notes

- To find out what it is worth, a business can use its balance sheet. This shows it how much it owns as against how much it owes. The balance sheet is often called a 'snapshot', as it shows the situation at the point in time at which it was taken. It can change very quickly.
- It is called the balance sheet because both sides must be equal. This is because they are measuring the same things. Think about what you own and owe. These are your assets and liabilities. The amount borrowed or earned to buy these assets must equal what you paid for them. It is the same with a business. There are three parts to a balance sheet. Each is linked to the others. They are:
  - *Assets* — all the things that the business owns as either fixed assets (non-current assets), such as buildings and machinery used in production, or current assets, such as stocks (inventories) of finished product that could be easily turned into cash.

Machinery is an example of an asset

Topic 46
Financial ratios

What the specification requires

You need to understand the purpose, calculation and interpretation of financial ratios. In other words, you need to know what financial ratios exist, and why they are used; how to calculate them from figures given; and what the resulting figures actually mean to the business.

In brief

Financial ratios are used by the stakeholders in a business to check on the financial efficiency and health of a business. They can be used to compare the business with previous time periods or with competitors. You may be asked to calculate ratios from figures you are given, but that should be easy because you will be provided with the formulae you need. The important thing is to be able to say what the ratios mean to that business, in that market. You may be asked to identify problems and provide possible solutions.

Revision notes

- **Financial ratios** are one of the tools used by stakeholders to judge the performance of a business. Businesses use them to find out how profitable and how solvent they are. The main purpose of working out financial ratios is as an aid to decision making.
- There are various profitability ratios, taken from information on the profit and loss account and the balance sheet.

Calculating financial ratios can give an idea of the health of the business

- **Gross profit margin** (gross profit to sales revenue) is measured as:

$$\frac{\text{gross profit}}{\text{turnover}} \times 100$$

- **Net profit margin** (net profit to sales revenue) takes overheads (expenses) into account and is measured as:

$$\frac{\text{net profit}}{\text{turnover}} \times 100$$

- **Return on capital employed** (or ROCE) compares the amount of profit made with the amount of money invested in the business. The higher the figure, the higher the return the investor is getting. Stakeholders can compare how well an investment is performing against other businesses or previous years. The formula is:

$$\frac{\text{net profit}}{\text{total capital employed}} \times 100$$

- Falling ratios indicate falling profitability and would be a signal that management needs to do something to cut costs or increase revenues.
- **Liquidity ratios** measure the short-term financial health of a business by looking at how capable it is of paying its short-term liabilities. They indicate whether the business is solvent. Two key ratios are:
  - **Current ratio** (working capital ratio) measures how many times over the company could pay its current liabilities from its current assets. It is calculated as:

$$\frac{\text{current assets}}{\text{current liabilities}}$$

  A healthy ratio would be in the region of 1.5:1 to 2:1.
  - **Acid test ratio** measures how many times over the company could pay its current liabilities from its current assets even if stock remained unsold. This is a much sterner test of the ability of the business to pay debts. The formula is:

$$\frac{\text{current assets} - \text{stock}}{\text{current liabilities}}$$

Speak the language

acid test ratio — measures the same as current ratio, but disregards unsold stock

current ratio — how many times the company could pay its current liabilities from its current assets

financial ratios — show the relationships between key parts of the business's accounts

gross profit margin — measures the profitability of a business in relation to its turnover

liquidity ratios — measure the ability of the business to pay its debts

net profit margin — measures the profitability of a business, after expenses, in relation to its turnover

return on capital employed — compares the amount of profit made with the amount of money invested in the business

The paper is marked out of 90 and you have 1 hour in which to complete it. Remember that papers will not cover the whole of the content, but will choose to concentrate on different content each year. The paper has some background information and Items for you to use. Papers will not always be based on a single business.

Background information

Webbs is a small private printing business. It prints football programmes, leaflets and brochures, and school and college publications, such as prospectuses. It has two large machines (for different types of printing), two full-time employees as well as Mr Webb and one part-time employee, who carries out administrative duties.

1 (a) **Webbs faces various costs, but is not sure into which categories they fall. State whether each of the following is a fixed, variable or semi-variable cost.**
   (i) **Rent for the premises**
   (ii) **Paper for printing**
   (iii) **Ink for printing**
   (iv) **Maintenance of machinery**
   (v) **Business rates**
   (vi) **Fuel for delivery vehicles** *(6 marks)*

(b) **Mr Webb is trying to see if a new machine he could buy to print small runs of leaflets will break even. The fixed costs for the machine are £300. Variable costs are £20. The least he can sell the output for is £80. Calculate breakeven using the formula:**

$$\text{breakeven} = \frac{\text{fixed costs}}{\text{selling price} - \text{variable cost}}$$

(3 marks)

(c) **An increase in business rates has increased Webbs' costs. Explain how this increase would affect breakeven.** *(5 marks)*

(d) **Given the new level of fixed costs, Webbs will struggle to reach breakeven. Using the information given and your own knowledge, suggest, with examples, what Mr Webb could do to improve the situation.** *(12 marks)*

(e) **Which improvement would you recommend? Give reasons for your answer.** *(4 marks)*

Total: 30 marks

2 Mr Webb has drawn up a cash-flow forecast for the final 3 months of the year, based on last year. This is a busy time of year for football programmes and for programmes and brochures for school fairs and productions. He notes that, although he has a cash surplus at the end of the year, he has had constant deficits up to December.

(a) Explain what is meant by a 'cash surplus' and what effect this could have on the business. *(3 marks)*

(b) Suggest and explain THREE actions that Mr Webb could take to deal with his company's constant cash-flow deficits. *(9 marks)*

(c) Webbs' gross profit margin is 21% and its operating margin 2%.
(i) Suggest what these figures indicate. *(8 marks)*
(ii) Suggest what action Mr Webb should be taking as a result of these figures. *(4 marks)*

Total: 24 marks

3 Below is part of the balance sheet for Webbs.

Fixed assets (non-current assets)	£
Land and buildings	50,000
Printing machinery	30,000
Vehicles	20,000
Computers	10,000
Furniture and fittings	10,000
(Total fixed assets)	?
Current assets	
Stocks (inventories)	10,000
Debtors (receivables)	45,000
Cash	5,000
(Subtotal of current assets)	?
Current liabilities	
Creditors (payables)	40,000
Bank overdraft	10,000
Tax owed	5,000
(Subtotal of current liabilities)	?
Net current assets (working capital)	
Current assets minus current liabilities	?
Net assets employed	
Fixed assets plus net current assets	?

(a) Calculate and complete the missing figures. *(5 marks)*

(b) Using the formulae:

$$\text{current ratio} = \frac{\text{current assets}}{\text{current liabilities}}$$

$$\text{acid test ratio} = \frac{\text{current assets} - \text{stock}}{\text{current liabilities}}$$

calculate the current ratio and acid test ratio. *(6 marks)*

(c) Suggest what ratios at this level mean for Webbs. What action would you recommend as a result of calculating these ratios? *(9 marks)*

Total: 20 marks

4 Mr Webb currently operates the business as a sole trader. He is thinking of turning the business into a private limited company. This would allow him to raise the finance for the machine through the sale of shares.

(a) Advise Mr Webb on which form of ownership would be best suited to his aims. Give reasons for your answer. *(9 marks)*

(b) Mr Webb could also try to raise the money from a venture capitalist. Explain what is meant by 'venture capitalist'. Use your own knowledge and any information you have on Webbs to explain whether one would be interested in this business. *(7 marks)*

Total: 16 marks

Overall total: 90 marks

Controlled assessment

Advice on controlled assessment

A controlled assessment is a new type of assessment that is replacing coursework. It tests the same sorts of skills as coursework used to test, but under conditions that are more controlled. Controlled assessments are designed to be:

- researched independently
- completed during lessons within a set time
- supervised during the final write-up

There is a recommended time for research and for the final write-up for each assessment. This means that, with most assessments, you can undertake the research at home, or in a library, or on the internet. You can then use this research to help you with your final write-up. You can take a folder or portfolio of your research into the classroom when you are doing your final write-up.

Your teacher can give you feedback on your choice of business, on the focus you have chosen and on the sort of research that you are undertaking. This must all take place before the final write-up.

The final stage is a supervised period to write up your research findings. This can be spread across a number of sessions. You are advised to spend around 17 hours on the research and 7 hours on the write-up. Your teacher will supervise this stage.

The controlled assessment units you attempt will depend on the qualification route you have decided:

- If you are taking the short course, you will take Unit 14: Investigating Small Businesses.
- If you are taking the full course, you will take Unit 3: Investigating Small Businesses.
- If you are taking the double award Applied course, you will take two of Unit 4: People in Business; Unit 5: Marketing and Customer Needs; or Unit 6: Enterprise.

Advice on specific units

Unit 3 and Unit 14

Investigating Small Businesses: these units are identical but numbered differently depending on which route you are taking. A scenario is set each year by the examination board for you to investigate. The specimen material produced by AQA gives the following example and advice:

Advice on Unit 4

People in Business covers essential knowledge of business structures and employees necessary for you to begin to consider your future career. You choose a business and investigate and report on how it is organised, the job roles within it, and the specific working arrangements at three different levels within the business — manager, supervisor and employee. You investigate the practical aspects of employee motivation in your chosen business. You should show a clear understanding of the way the people within a business work for and with each other and apply this knowledge to managers, supervisors and employees. You should consider whether you would want to work for this business by looking at your own skills. You will especially look at team skills and your own personality, using personality tests.

Advice on Unit 5

Marketing and Customer Needs investigates how businesses use marketing activities to meet customers' needs and to deal with competition. You will investigate, and report on, how businesses carry out customer research — how they identify customers and their key characteristics, and how they then attempt to meet customer needs. You will study and investigate the practical ways in which businesses attempt to gain competitive advantage through the elements of the marketing mix. You should investigate the meaning of customer service and its importance, and evaluate how businesses decide on levels of customer service. In particular, you should understand how businesses use ICT and new technology to monitor and improve customer service.

Advice on Unit 6

Enterprise offers candidates the opportunity to set up, run and reflect on the success of an enterprise activity. It encourages you to develop and explore the attributes associated with enterprise and entrepreneurship by planning, implementing and evaluating an enterprise activity. It gives a broad overview of enterprise skills that are present in successful entrepreneurs, and shows that enterprise skills are found not only in businesses but also in social enterprises.

You will set up and run a small enterprise by identifying and selecting a business opportunity, conducting market research and writing a business plan. You will then implement the enterprise outlined in your business plan, subject to external and internal influences.

Finally, you will write up an in-depth evaluation of your individual team role as well as that of your group. This is finished off with an action plan for both your personal development and the possible development of the business.

Speak the language index